BRIA

Acting

Brian O'Neil is a former talent agent and personal
manager who has represented actors for theater, film,
television, commercials, and radio. As a talent representative, he was responsible for the career guidance
and professional placement for hundreds of actors.
He is the founder of Acting as a Business, a one-on-
one, career-consultation and career-coaching service
for actors. He lives in New York City and is a
frequent guest lecturer at some of the nation's finest
acting-training programs including the Yale School
of Drama and the Juilliard School.

www.actingasabusiness.com

Acting as a Business

Acting as a Business

Strategies for Success

BRIAN O'NEIL

Fourth Edition

VINTAGE BOOKS

A Division of Random House, Inc.

New York

FIRST VINTAGE BOOKS EDITION, OCTOBER 2009

Library of Congress Cataloging-in-Publication Data:
O'Neil, Brian.
Acting as a business : strategies for success / by Brian O'Neil.—4th ed.,
1st Vintage Books ed.
p.   cm.
ISBN 978-0-307-47392-9
1. Acting—Vocational guidance—United States.   I. Title.
PN2055.O54 2009
792.02'8'023—dc22
2009015191

www.vintagebooks.com

Printed in the United States of America
10   9   8   7   6   5   4   3   2

For my wonderful parents—
my mother, Aileen Therese O'Neil,
and my father, Joseph Patrick O'Neil

For my wonderful parents—
my mother, Aileen Therese O'Neil,
and my father, Joseph Patrick O'Neil

Contents

Acknowledgments

For their assistance and support in this fourth edition of *Acting as a Business: Strategies for Success,* there are many people to whom I am indebted and to whom I wish to express my gratitude. Thank you Anthony Gentile, Donna Daley, Robert Rigley, Rosemary Keough, Paul dePasquale, Stephen Gregory, Brick Karnes, Scott Comin, Anthony Cistaro, Josh Casaubon, Jason Nuzzo, Jason Milton, Lorraine Gracey, Ben Curtis, Kyle Zingler, Tony Vincent, Lisa Gold, Tony Nation, Paul Michael, Lanie Zipoy, Tom Rowen, Max Van Bel, Catherine Weidner, Brandon Ruckdashel, Terry Schreiber, Matt Jared, Zachary Wagman, Holly Lebed, Jane Kronick, Jeffrey Gill, Robin Dornbaum, Jenny Carbone, Marilynn Zitner, Claudia Black, Lisa Beach, Jane Jenkins, JoAnna Beckson, Ron Stetson, Michael Howard, Jack Newman, Larry Singer, David Alan Basche, Mary Harden, Nancy Curtis, Josh Radnor, Eric Millegan, Colin O'Leary, Sam Chwat, Sherry Eaker, Dan Mason, Lois Goodwin, Arline McGovern, Tess Steinkolk, Robert Todd,

Lydia Laurans, Barry Shapiro, Janis Dardaris, Andrea Frierson, Tim Phillips, Kevin Brunnock, Jacob Harran, Susan Varon, Steven Harris, Ellen Orchid, Sara Krieger, Mimi Hines, Flo Rothacker, Scott Glasgow, Joan See, and Melanie Baker.

For their continued support of my work with their students—I am grateful to: Katherine Hood and Jerry Shafnisky of the Drama Division at the Juilliard School; Kyle Donnelly, Charlie Oates, and Linn Fridy at the University of California, San Diego; Evan Yionoulis and James Bundy at the Yale School of Drama; Daniel Renner, Jennifer Forsyth, and Marti Steger at the National Theatre Conservatory at the Denver Center for the Performing Arts; Ray Dooley at the University of North Carolina, Chapel Hill; Stephen Berenson and Brian McEleny at Brown University/Trinity Rep Consortium; Richard Seer at the University of San Diego/Old Globe Theatre; Donna Snow, Roberta Sloan, and David Ingram at Temple University; Lisa Nicholas at Syracuse University; John David Lutz at the University of Evansville; and Deborah White McEniry at Anderson University.

Thank you also to my mentors (and friends) Steve Carson and the late Fifi Oscard who taught me everything and entrusted me with so much responsibility so early on. Thanks to Matthew Broderick and Meg Ryan and to my agents (and friends) Barbara Hogenson and Nicole Verity at the Barbara Hogenson Agency.

A very special thanks to Lisa A. Barnett for her invaluable suggestions, guidance, warmth, and humor. And for their ongoing support, my gratitude to Kerry, Chris, Marie, Michael, Cheryl, Joe, and Liz O'Neil.

And to the many actors it has been my pleasure to know, my friends and clients—you have enriched my life. Thanks to you all.

Author's Note

I'd like to say thank you to the acting communities of New York, Los Angeles, and everywhere in between for having made the first three editions of *Acting as a Business: Strategies for Success*—successful! After selling through twenty-five printings, we now have a completely revised and updated fourth edition.

I have two minor revisions left to make, and I have saved them especially for this space. In the introduction, you'll read that the information in this book is based on my "twenty years of experience in the entertainment industry." That's now thirty years. The introduction will also tell you that I've held "over one thousand private, in-depth career planning and counseling sessions." Make that *four* thousand.

The latter point is crucial. Most of you who have met me since the first edition was printed have reinforced and reassured me of what I already knew to be true: *These ideas work.*

There's something else. Over the past several years many

actors have told me that *Acting as a Business inspired* them. It was never my intention to inspire, only to *inform*. However, if these words also serve to inspire you, all the better.

For best results, I recommend reading the book in its entirety before implementing any of the ideas or strategies I have outlined. And if there are topics you'd like to see covered in subsequent editions, or if you are looking for information pertaining to my services, please contact me at the website address below:

www.actingasabusiness.com

Introduction

Certainly, there has been no dearth of books written on the subjects of starting an acting career or breaking into show business. And much has already been said regarding the need for quality training, "proper" photographs, and resume format. And, of course, we have been repeatedly treated to the time-worn admonition that show business is a *business,* and that perhaps more than talent and luck, the trait most necessary for success is persistence.

What has not been written, to the best of my knowledge, are words that instruct the actor in specific methods and strategies that the actor can implement to create career-advancing opportunities. In other words, actors have not been taught *how* to persist.

Some years ago, when I was an actor myself, a famous casting director said to me, "You have to bug these agents and

casting directors! Bug them, in a *good* way, I mean!" This
seemed to me, contradictory. "Bug them in a *good* way"? What
did this mean? It haunted me! Later, as a talent agent, I would
discover what it meant. And *still* I would have to bug people—
bug them to audition my clients—if I was to thrive as an agent.
What words would open doors for the clients I represented? I
was soon to learn! In the manner that agents speak to casting
directors, directors, and producers on behalf of their clients, so
must the actor learn to speak to agents, casting directors, directors, etc., on their own behalf. But actors often don't know how
best to communicate, because they are often unaware of specifically what those with whom they are communicating need.
Therefore, much of this book concerns *communication*—both
spoken and written—that most clearly and effectively makes
an impact on both those who represent actors and those who
hire them. The book also details resources by which an actor
can research and gain access to necessary casting information—
well in advance of the casting process. Perhaps most importantly, this book will teach the actor how to *ask* for what he or
she wants from those in a position to give it.

The information in this book is based on twenty years of
experience in the entertainment industry: as an actor, as well as
a talent agent and personal manager who represented actors in
the areas of theater, film, television, commercials, and radio.
These observations also come from the over one thousand private, in-depth career-planning and counseling sessions I have
had over several years with actors at every career level. This is
my perspective.

Regardless of the level of success one achieves, a career as an
actor is never an easy one. But I intend to dispel myths born
out of excuses, and festered by negative thinking—the dead-

liest of diseases to the spirit of any performing artist. I will also talk about the areas that I have found to be the most common stumbling blocks for the actor. In several cases, I have changed a name or a title to keep the confidence of those who have been generous enough to let me tell their stories, or who have allowed me to invade their privacy.

Since much of the book concerns correspondence, I had best immediately dispel the first myth: Agents and casting directors, as well as other entertainment business personnel, get their mail—and they read it, too! Every agent and casting director with whom I have been acquainted—and there are many—reads their mail. Now they may not always admit this to actors, but on the whole, they are indeed reading it. The reports I get every week from my clients' response to their mailings verifies this further.

Since I will say little beyond this point regarding the actor's need to maintain a healthy state of mind, let me hang out my shingle for a moment and express my thoughts on this topic, as the book's subject matter is strongly linked to it. In this profession of acting, it is especially difficult to feel a sense of control over one's career. The actor is constantly at the mercy of those who make decisions concerning his or her immediate, and sometimes long-range, fate. Critical to our sense of well-being and happiness, however, is a feeling of having some control over our lives. By setting goals, making plans, and organizing our strategies, we are exercising control. We feel better. By recording our thoughts, writing down the actions we plan to take, and reading over even our most incremental progress and small achievements, our self-esteem grows. Risk becomes a little easier, and we summon the courage we need to get up to bat one more time.

It is the talented and committed actors—the beginners, as well as the not-so-new, who know that acting is a business, and that persistence is a necessity, but who don't always know the inroads or the resources that can help to make persistence a more bearable burden—for whom I have written this book.

Acting as a
Business.

1

From Stage to Screen

Recently, I was invited to address the graduating class of a top conservatory training program for actors in New York City. I asked the group to give a few minutes of thought to where they would like to see themselves professionally in five years' time. Then I asked for a show of hands from all those who were thinking in terms of "film." Every hand in the group, except one, shot up. The one holdout responded "theater *and* film."

Prior to the above-mentioned speaking engagement, I was a guest at another well-known acting training program, also in New York City, where I posed the same question to a theater full of young acting students. And got essentially the same response—mostly "film," several "television," and only a few "theater."

In the past, an actor seeking a career in film or television usually ventured west to Hollywood while the actor pursuing work in the theater migrated to New York. The westward trek is still made, but it has become equally true that most young actors who come to New York are also eyeing careers in film or television. This has become the ultimate goal, or dream, for most of the actors with whom I come in contact.

Why this change? One major contribution to the powerful lure of the film and television industry is a now decentralized theater scene, which makes it necessary for most actors to accept often low-paying out-of-town engagements if they are to be employed in the theater at all. Yet, despite the hardships, there is still probably no better way for the New York actor who seeks a career in film or television to give this dream a chance than to strive for the highest quality visibility possible in the theater. With models, child actors, teenage actors, and actors still youthful enough to convincingly portray teenage characters comprising the main exceptions, the overwhelming majority of film and television careers born out of New York are of actors who have first been seen on the stage.

Why is this so? Mainly, for two reasons: visibility and credibility. First, let's talk about *visibility*. When a play opens on or off-Broadway and receives good notices, it is the actors in this play whom the film and television industries—such as they exist in New York—see. Literally. A big part of the jobs of those who cast is to be aware of which actors are being praised for their performances, and to see their work. In turn, it is these actors who are often requested to audition for, and then frequently land, roles in film and television productions that are being cast in New York. This is especially true in television, where there is a continual demand for new and ongoing programming. Not only does New York now boast several hit prime-time series of its own, but there is also pilot season—the bulk of which takes place in the first four months of the year. It is at this time when Hollywood casting executives visiting the east are able to see the New York talent pool. From this talent pool, a number of actors will be cast in leading and supporting roles in television pilots, the most well received of which are then developed as new series for the upcoming television season.

And where do television casting personnel go to find the New York actors who will be auditioned for these new pilots? Mainly, to the theater. They attend the hit shows of the current season. An examination of the upcoming fall television season in any given year will usually boast several actors who made a splash in the previous New York theater season. In fact, the annual prime-time Emmy Award nominee roster often contains the names of a number of actors who were nominated for—or in some cases have even won—a Tony Award in the theatrical season or two prior to becoming known to national television audiences.

Earlier, I mentioned that the stage is the likeliest route to film and prime-time television success for the *New York* actor. Film and prime-time success, without benefit of a stage career, is more common in Los Angeles, where much of the casting is done according to "look" and "type." Many actors who find good representation on the West Coast—which is no easy feat in itself—are subsequently auditioned and cast in films and television. While working in the theater is certainly advantageous to the Los Angeles actor, it is not necessarily the prerequisite route to film and prime-time television that it so often is in New York.

While some might observe that New York comedy clubs have long been choice spots for discovery by the film and television industry, two things must be pointed out. First, the career path of a New York comic who becomes a success in either film or prime-time television usually goes first from the comedy club stage to talk shows, comedy, or variety television (such as *Saturday Night Live*, *The Late Show with David Letterman*, etc.). From this exposure, the comic may then go on to work in film or prime-time television. Second, while an individual comic's background may not include the theater, per se, the comic's talents have still come to the attention of the film and television industry first through the comic's visibility on the *stage*.

In *daytime* television, more specifically soap operas, young actors on both coasts are often cast in contract roles without benefit of a career in the theater. This is not to say that the young actors who are selected for soap opera roles are without training or talent, merely that they tend to be blessed with uncommon good looks—usually a primary consideration in the casting of these roles.

Earlier, I mentioned that actors in New York who succeed in film or prime-time television *without* benefit of a stage career are generally those who land a sizable role in a film or television series while still very young. The reason for this is quite simple. Very few actors at such an early age will have had the opportunity to build a highly visible career in the theater—nor are there very many roles for child or teen actors in most new plays. Therefore, casting directors will frequently audition relatively inexperienced young actors who have already found representation, or perhaps have come to their attention by way of a referral. This is sometimes a necessity in order to find the right actors who are young enough to convincingly portray the characters in the roles being cast. And so, New York has spawned the careers of such popular stars as Tom Cruise, Meg Ryan, Elisabeth Shue, Uma Thurman, Matt Dillon, Christina Ricci, Kirsten Dunst, Rosario Dawson, Chloe Sevigny, Ashton Kutcher, Michelle Rodriguez, and Julia Roberts—to name a few—all of whose careers began in New York without visibility in the theater. All of the above landed a leading or supporting role in a film or prime-time television series while they were still not past the age of twenty-one.

On the other hand, when a play featuring a child or a teenage character is a success, the young actor playing the role will oftentimes find himself in immediate demand by the film and television industry. Historically, this has always been the case, and continues to be so. Let's take a look back at some prime examples from the past two decades. The 1980s Neil Simon hit *Brighton Beach Memoirs* launched the film career of Matthew Broderick along with the careers of a host of other young actors who succeeded him in the course of the play's three-year run. This list includes: Fisher Stevens, Jon Cryer, Robert Sean Leonard, Patrick Dempsey, and Jonathan Silverman. As each of these unknowns assumed the lead role of Eugene, his visibility and credibility escalated enormously. Throughout the '80s many other teen and pre-teen actors rose through the ranks by appearing in productions both on and off-Broadway. Some of these "kids" were: Macaulay Culkin (off-Broadway in the Ensemble Studio Theater's production of *After School Special*); Sarah Michelle Gellar (off-Broadway in *The Widow Claire* at Circle-in-the-Square); Jennifer Aniston (in the New York Shakespeare Festival's production of *For Dear Life*); and future Oscar winner Adrien Brody—at the ripe old age of thirteen—appeared off-Broadway in *Family Pride in the '50s*. At fifteen, Brody would become a regular on the short-lived Mary Tyler Moore series *Annie McGuire*.

The 1990s rolled in and the "junior" division was represented by many, including a pre-teen (and pre-film) Natalie Portman in the off-Broadway hit *Ruthless!* That same year, an eight-year-old unknown named Scarlett Johansson debuted at

Playwrights Horizons in *Sophistry.* The later-to-become-star of ABC's *Teen Angel,* Mike Damus, understudied on Broadway in Neil Simon's *Lost in Yonkers,* and another then unknown teen—*Dawson's Creek* star James Van Der Beek—launched his career off-Broadway at the Signature Theater Company in Edward Albee's *Finding the Sun.* Eddie Kay Thomas understudied in the Lincoln Center production of John Guare's *Four Baboons Adoring the Sun* and later appeared on Broadway in the 1999 revival of *The Diary of Anne Frank.* Thomas would later co-star in such films as *American Pie* and the WB series *Off Centre.* Teenage unknown Michael Pitt appeared off-Broadway at the prestigious New York Theatre Workshop in *The Trestle at Pope Lick Creek* and immediately thereafter was cast in a recurring role on *Dawson's Creek.* Pitt would later star in such films as John Cameron Mitchell's *Hedwig and the Angry Inch* and Bernardo Bertolucci's *The Dreamers.* Nine-year-old Mischa Barton appeared off-Broadway in Pulitzer Prize–winning playwright Tony Kushner's *Slavs.* Later, Ms. Barton would perform at Lincoln Center in James Lapine's *Twelve Dreams* and in two productions at the New York Shakespeare Festival. Eventually, Ms. Barton would become the co-star of the hit Fox series *The O.C.*

The "adult" division found Billy Crudup in Lincoln Center's *Arcadia,* Taye Diggs in *Rent,* and a pre–*Dharma and Greg's* Thomas Gibson performing both on Broadway and off. Jennifer Garner understudied on Broadway in *A Month in the Country,* and an unknown Jude Law appeared opposite Kathleen Turner on Broadway in *Indiscretions.* The soon-to-be star of ABC's *The Practice,* Camryn Manheim, won praise for her one-woman off-Broadway hit *Wake Up, I'm Fat.* Another unknown named Michael Emerson appeared onstage in *Gross Indecency: The Three Trials of Oscar Wilde* and would later join

Manheim as a cast member of *The Practice*. Manhattan Theatre Club's production of Terrence McNally's *Love! Valour! Compassion!* positioned actor Justin Kirk to nab a co-starring role on the WB series *Jack and Jill;* Kirk would later co-star in HBO's *Angels in America*. It was also at Manhattan Theatre Club where Debra Messing understudied in John Patrick Shanley's *Four Dogs and a Bone*. Ms. Messing later co-starred in the off-Broadway production *Collected Stories* and then became the co-star of such series as *Ned and Stacey* and *Will & Grace*. At approximately the same time, Vera Farmiga understudied on Broadway in *Taking Sides*. Shortly thereafter, Ms. Farmiga would become the co-star of the Fox series *Roar* opposite the late Heath Ledger. Ms. Farmiga would then go on to become the star of numerous feature films including *The Departed*.

From the late '90s through 2009, we have watched many stage actors make the transition from stage to screen. David Alan Basche bounced from off-Broadway successes *Visiting Mr. Green* and *Snakebit* to become the co-star of the hit NBC series *Three Sisters* and the feature film *War of the Worlds*. Allison Janney won a Tony Award for her performance in the Broadway revival of Arthur Miller's *A View from the Bridge* and would then go on to co-star in the series *The West Wing*. Also appearing regularly on *The West Wing* was Kristin Chenoweth, Tony winner of the hit revival of *You're a Good Man, Charlie Brown*. Ms. Chenoweth would later become a star of the series *Pushing Daisies,* where she would be joined as a series regular by Lee Pace, who had previously appeared in a Playwrights Horizons production called *The Credeaux Canvas*.

Good fortune struck other actors appearing in a more recent off-Broadway play by Terrence McNally entitled *Corpus Christi*. This production showcased the talent of actors Anson Mount and Sean Dugan. Mount would go on to star in several films including *Urban Legends: The Final Cut,* and Dugan would appear regularly on the HBO series *Oz.* Stephanie March, featured in the Broadway revival of *Death of a Salesman* would soon become a regular on the hit series *Law and Order: Special Victims Unit,* and Dagmara Dominczyk, who understudied on Broadway in *Closer,* would be cast in lead roles in such films as *The Count of Monte Cristo.* Young actor Eddie Cahill appeared off-Broadway at the Vineyard Theatre in Nicky Silver's *The Altruist;* as a result Cahill would guest star on *Sex and the City,* land a recurring role on *Friends,* and co-star with Kurt Russell in the film *Miracle.* Shortly thereafter Cahill would become a regular on the series *CSI: New York.*

A short while later, an unknown Dallas Roberts appeared in Maria Irene Fornes's *Enter the Night* at the Signature Theatre Company, while a few blocks away Derek Richardson was making his professional acting debut at the "A-list" off-Broadway theater Playwrights Horizons in Kira Obolensky's *Lobster Alice.* As an immediate and direct result, Richardson made guest appearances on several prime-time series and then was cast in a starring role in the film *Dumb and Dumberer: When Harry Met Lloyd.* Later he would become the co-star of the series *Men in Trees,* and Dallas Roberts would go on to appear in such films as *A Home at the End of the World,* in which he co-starred with Colin Farrell. At exactly the same time, newcomer Eric Millegan appeared in the Broadway revival of Andrew Lloyd Webber's *Jesus Christ Superstar.* Immediately thereafter, Millegan was cast in the lead role in the independent film *On_Line* and later became a regular on the hit Fox series *Bones.*

Danny Pino co-starred with the earlier mentioned Billy Crudup in the New York Shakespeare Festival's production of *Measure for Measure* and was then cast in a starring role on the WB series *Men, Women, and Dogs.* Later, Pino would become a series regular on CBS's prime-time series *Cold Case*. After appearing in the hit revival of *Noises Off,* actor T. R. Knight became a regular on Nathan Lane's series *Charlie Lawrence* and later would become a co-star of the hit series *Grey's Anatomy.* Young actress Ashley Williams understudied in the off-Broadway hit *The Shape of Things.* Shortly thereafter Ms. Williams would become the co-star of the hit NBC series *Good Morning, Miami.* There she would be joined by Mark Feurstein, who had previously appeared at off-Broadway's prestigious Classic Stage Company. Patrick Wilson starred in Broadway's *The Full Monty* and would later be nominated for an Emmy for his performance in HBO's *Angels in America* and then star in such films as *Little Children* and *Watchmen.* Also appearing in the stage version of *Monty* was ten-year-old newcomer Conor Paolo, who would later become a series regular on the CW hit *Gossip Girl.*

The Broadway revival of *Cabaret* led Michael C. Hall to a starring role on HBO's *Six Feet Under,* and Roger Bart of Broadway's blockbuster hit *The Producers* was prominently cast in the remake of *The Stepford Wives* with Nicole Kidman. Multiple Tony Award winners Audra McDonald and Donna Murphy were further "awarded"—Ms. McDonald with a role as a series regular on the NBC prime-time show *Mr. Sterling* and Ms. Murphy with a co-starring role in the smash hit film *Spider-Man 2.* Tony nominee Daniel Sunjata of the Richard Greenberg prize-winning play *Take Me Out* became the star of the series *Rescue Me,* and after an understudying assignment in the hit Broadway play *Proof,* Andrea Anders appeared in a lead role in the Broadway version of *The Graduate.* Before long, Ms. Anders would become the co-star of the *Friends* spinoff series *Joey.* After appearing in leading roles on Broadway in *Epic Proportions* and off-Broadway in Paul Rudnick's *The Most Fabulous*

Story Ever Told, Alan Tudyk became the star of such films as *I, Robot, Dodgeball,* and *Serenity.*

Mid to late in the first decade of the new century, many more actors made the stage-to-screen transition: The CBS series *The Class* boasted three regulars who had just performed lead roles in Broadway hits: Julie Halston of *Hairspray;* Jesse Tyler Ferguson of *Spelling Bee;* and Heather Goldenhersh of the John Patrick Shanley Pulitzer Prize–winning play *Doubt.* Newcomer Oscar Isaac, who had recently appeared in the New York Shakespeare Festival's productions of *Two Gentlemen of Verona* and *Romeo and Juliet* as well as the play *Beauty of the Father* at Manhattan Theatre Club, would go on to co-star with Leonardo DiCaprio and Russell Crowe in the feature film *Body of Lies.* Rutina Wesley, after appearing in the Broadway production of David Hare's *The Vertical Hour,* was cast in a starring role in the film *How She Move* and then became a series regular on HBO's *True Blood.* And on and on it goes.

Why is this? Besides the relatively simple and logical "theory of visibility," there is, as I mentioned earlier, the matter of *credibility.* In addition to a widely held belief that the true test of an actor's ability can be seen on the stage, it is important to realize how much pre-screening the actor goes through before being selected for a role at this professional level. Usually, his photo and resume are first reviewed by the play's casting director. The casting director does not actually cast the production. Casting directors are hired by producers and directors for their thorough knowledge of the acting community, as well as for their discerning tastes in talent. The casting director describes in detail the various roles available in a printed, daily outline—to which agents subscribe—called Breakdown Services. Besides auditioning actors selected from the submissions made by agents, the casting director also holds open auditions for members of Actors' Equity Association, the specific details of which are listed in the casting sections of trade publications.

After successfully auditioning for the casting director, an actor may then be called back for subsequent auditions for the director, the producer, and the playwright. It is this trio who will make the final casting decisions. By the time the actor wins the role, and achieves this prized visibility, he has usually passed many tests, and has been selected over many other actors.

An understudy has credibility simply by association with the hit play, as he too has probably passed many tests. His agent, if he has one, will probably have an easier time getting him seen by film and television casting personnel who may previously have overlooked him. Even without performing the role, this high-level understudy assignment is a strong "selling point." If the actor is without an agent, he may soon find himself represented, either by inviting agents to see him—if he does perform—or by being granted interviews on the basis of this newly acquired status. This is credibility.

Amazingly, as we shall see in detail in Chapters 5 and 6, if an actor is even being called back to audition further for a role in which he is ultimately not cast, he still establishes a potentially very powerful credibility.

None of the foregoing is meant to imply in any way, however, that if an actor achieves this level of visibility, he is assured of "crossing over" to a career in film or prime-time television. Far from it. It is simply to explain how the stage-to-screen process takes place in New York. Many talented and committed actors have found themselves employed in film and television simply as a *result* of their work on the stage. In other words, the industry found *them*. I cannot overemphasize this point, as it eludes so many actors. If you have your doubts on this score, leaf through some past volumes of John Willis's *The-*

atre World, which has been in publication for nearly fifty years. Available at many libraries, this annual pictorial contains photos and cast lists of Broadway, off-Broadway, national touring companies, and regional theater productions. On page after page of these books, you will find photos of currently popular film and television stars who were then coming to the attention of the industry that would make them famous. An Internet search will yield similar results.

There is a true, yet somewhat misleading, notion that stars from film and television are offered the best stage roles. There is no doubt that producers very often do look for actors with name recognition to fill the lead roles in New York stage productions. However, many of these stars who appear on and off-Broadway are merely *returning* to the scene that helped to launch their film and television careers in the first place. In recent seasons, the New York theater has welcomed home such "brand names" as Gene Hackman, Bebe Neuwirth, Meryl Streep, Richard Dreyfuss, Jason Biggs, Martin Sheen, Dustin Hoffman, Kathleen Turner, Marilu Henner, Glenn Close, Tyne Daly, David Hyde Pierce, Judd Hirsch, Christian Slater, Jane Fonda, Jon Voight, Kevin Bacon, and many other veterans of the New York stage.

This "trend" is not as new as many believe. In the 1960s through '80s alone, Broadway was regularly populated with stars from film and television—many so popular they arrived with recent Oscars and Emmys in tow—others were nothing short of legends in their own time. Among those appearing in plays and musicals in New York at that time were Katharine Hepburn, Bette Davis, Henry Fonda, Kirk Douglas, Danny Kaye, Rod Steiger, Anne Bancroft, Charlton Heston, Tallulah Bankhead, Vivien Leigh, Paul Newman, Joanne Woodward, George C. Scott, E. G. Marshall, Shirley Booth, Sammy Davis,

Jr., Jackie Gleason, Art Carney, Mary Tyler Moore, Liza Minnelli, Sandy Dennis, Lucille Ball, Sandy Duncan, Shelley Winters, Lee Grant, Peter Falk, and on and on and on. Then, as now, in many cases, the stars were returning to the scene that made their careers in film and television happen. Many New York actors feel that if they could get film and television recognition, they would then be able to get great stage roles. While this is so, if one is a New York actor, then usually one must make one's mark in the theater first. And sought after though they may be, *most* stars who are currently popular in film or television express little interest in working in the New York theater. Lower earnings, the time commitment necessary, and the drudgery—real or perceived—of performing eight shows per week, all add up to a situation that is less than enticing for the actor who is currently a hot property in Hollywood. Surprising as it may seem, at the time of this writing, of the performers who are currently making their living on the New York stage, fewer than three percent are known to film and television audiences. Stars of film and television who seek work in the New York theater are the *exceptions,* which is fortunate for the New York stage actor, for if things were as some say, there would be no work available at all for the actor who is not already well known.

It must also be remembered that in many cases, especially revivals, a production might not get mounted at all, if stars were not appearing in the lead roles. Remember, too, that most of the remainder of the cast, who will be playing supporting and minor roles, will not be actors who are known by the film and television industry. These actors will now have the opportunity to be seen by film and television casting personnel—and some will become stars themselves. Simply put, it is the stage—most notably Broadway, off-Broadway, and in these early years of the twenty-first century, even the very finest off-off-Broadway theater companies—where the film and television industry is most likely to discover the New York actor—both who he is and what he can do.

Theater. Film. Television. New York. Los Angeles.

How does the actor who aspires to a career in any of these areas, or either of these cities, prepare to give this dream a chance? First, let's assemble some basic essentials—photos and resumes—and then we'll talk about learning how to create career-building opportunities.

2

The Arsenal

PHOTOGRAPHS

East Coast or West, there are some materials an actor must have before setting out to explore new territories and create opportunities. First, is the photograph. Due to its highly subjective nature, there is probably little in the ongoing course of an actor's career that holds greater potential for disparity of opinion than the actor's selection of the "right" photographs. More to the point, pursuit of the photograph that will please all is futile. Despite the professional expertise of any one viewer, there will rarely be complete agreement as to which photos, and of course, which photographers, are best. Therefore, a preoccupation with this subject is, at best, time-wasting. Carried to the extreme, it can be enough to drive you—and those to whom you send the online link to your latest set of proofs—to utter distraction. And yet, undeniably, having "good" photographs is a necessity. What, then, constitutes a good photograph? Obvious though it may seem, the basic prerequisite of a "good" photograph is that it must look like you. *Exactly.* The photograph should be of good quality, and it should make a statement about you. That is, it should capture some aspect of your personality, a definite expression, evident especially in the eyes.

In describing the "ideal" photograph, the words most commonly used by agents and casting directors alike are: "real," "natural," "warm," "energetic," "unretouched," "recent(!)," "relaxed," and always, always, "it must look exactly like you."

In choosing a photographer, first look at the photographs of actors you already know. Also visit one or two photo reproduction companies as listed in trade publications. It is the photo reproduction company that will make the copies of whichever photographs you ultimately choose to represent yourself. In New York and Los Angeles many reproduction companies (as well as photographers) advertise in *Back Stage* (see Appendix E). Most reproduction companies have on file rather extensive samplings of the work of currently popular photographers within your region. Most photographers also have websites for viewing samples of their work, as well. In these photo samplings note in particular those actors who are similar in age range and type to yourself.

Looking at these samplings will be invaluable in helping you get a sense of what constitutes overall "quality" in a photograph. It will allow you to see a volume of photographs, as well as the work of many photographers, in one sitting. Agents, casting directors, directors, and others who look at photographs of actors are used to seeing hundreds, even thousands of them. Sometimes at once. A photograph of less than first-rate quality, away from the context of other photographs, may seem fine to an actor; but to the knowing eye of an agent or casting director, the same photograph will be judged as outrageously bad. And while there will be endless opinions regarding your actual selection of a photograph, let's at least be sure the quality itself is excellent.

Telephone or email any photographers whose work you like, and ask to meet them in person. See how you like the photographer. It is critical that the photographer you select is someone with whom you feel comfortable. If you are to be "relaxed," "real," "natural," and other assorted adjectives that describe you at your best, certainly you will want to feel very much at ease with your photographer. In addition to questions about rates, and the number of pictures taken, be sure to ask about wardrobe. What about hair and makeup? Does the photographer have someone who will do this for you? What is the cost of this service? How much time will the photographer allow for the session?

Note the variety of styles in the photographers' samples. Commonly seen are wide-bordered photographs depicting more than just the actor's head, which was for decades the standard and accepted style, and known, unsurprisingly, as the "headshot." This newer trend is generally called the "portrait," and often includes up to three-quarters of the actor's body. For this reason, actors frequently, and erroneously, refer to this style as a "three-quarters shot." Properly, the term "three-quarters shot" refers to the angle and position of the photographic subject, not the amount of the actor's body that is depicted in the photo.

Flattering to actors whose faces look better at a distance, and especially becoming to those possessed of a great bod, the "portrait" trend remains popular, as does the headshot, only now photos are in color. While feelings toward the new style versus the old vary (of course!), one sentiment remains constant—your photographs must be about *you*. Your personality. Your essence. And—hopefully, anyway—your intelligence.

Specifically which photograph or photographs you select will depend on which markets you are approaching. I use the term "market" here to refer to any prospective buyer of your services as an actor. While many actors feel the need to make three different selections—a "commercial" shot, a "legit" shot, and a "soap" shot—the "soap" shot is not usually necessary, especially as it is so often found in the photographic arsenal of actors who have little potential for daytime television. Or at least not enough to warrant having a photograph specifically for that purpose.

What is meant by these three terms? The "commercial" photograph, often portraying a smiling actor radiating energy, can also be a more subtle image—as long as warmth is present. Despite the term "commercial," this photograph can often be used for many purposes besides the television commercial market alone. The "legit" shot, so called because it is generally geared toward the areas of legitimate theater, film, and television, is typified by a relaxed, natural, straightforward (not to be confused with *expressionless*) image of the actor. The "legit" shot captures its subject more in a state of repose than does the commercial shot. The so-called "soap" shot is typically a glamorous, romantic, strikingly dramatic photograph that looks, well, like someone on a soap opera. In most cases, however, the "legit" or "commercial" shot can be used for this purpose. While it is true that the denizens of dramatic daytime television dwell in a largely humorless world, they often possess dazzling smiles that enhance their beauty greatly. Therefore, a very attractive actor with a captivating smile would not necessarily be making a wrong choice—nor would their agent—by submitting the actor's "commercial" photograph to a soap opera's casting director. And certainly this smiling photograph would also be an appropriate selection for submission for many feature-length film, prime-time television (situation comedy, especially), and stage productions, as well.

Therefore, you will want to have an engaging and warm "commercial" photograph, as well as a more reposed, relaxed, and straightforward "legit" photograph in your arsenal in order to cover as broad a range of acting opportunities as you can. When you have made your selections, you will need at least fifty 8" × 10" copies of each photograph. Photo reproduction services that will also print your name on the front of your photograph are listed in *Back Stage* and other trade publications as well as on the Internet.

PHOTO POSTCARDS

In addition to 8" × 10" copies of your photos, you will also need to have a photo postcard made. Select the photograph that best typifies you, and lends itself to the markets you intend to pursue. You want this photo postcard to grab the attention of its recipient. In more cases than not, it is the "commercial" shot that makes the better photo postcard. The photo postcard, which is largely overused by actors, can, when used properly, serve a real function in conveying important information to those whom the actor is contacting. The most effective use of this postcard is, as we shall see—especially in the examples illustrated in Chapters 4 through 7—to show career progress, and build credibility in the eyes of those who can either hire you, or represent you for others to hire. On the back, as with a vacation postcard, write your message, or "progress report." On the front, under your photo, you can have your name, answering service, and union affiliations printed. Like your 8" × 10" photo reproductions, these postcards are available at photo reproduction centers listed in the trade papers and on the Internet as well.

RESUMES

The resume deserves far more attention than the actor usually gives it. With all the energy spent selecting the "right" photograph, it really is small wonder that so many do themselves a disservice where their resume is concerned. Consisting of a single page, and attached to the back of the photograph, your resume has precious little time to make an impact. That is why it must look perfect. Having a resume that looks perfect does not mean that you need to have amassed major stage credits or lead roles in television series. And while there is no one strict manner in which your resume must be formatted, three elements are essential. The perfect-looking resume is (1) laid out clearly, (2) concisely, and (3) without misrepresentation; it makes the most of your acting experience, training, and special skills. The perfect-looking resume welcomes the eye of its viewer.

My first suggestion for a "viewer-friendly" resume is to have it printed on *off-white* paper, such as ivory, cream, or light gray. Costing only pennies more than white copy paper, off-white or grey reduces the glare of the harsh office light in which your resume is all-too-quickly reviewed. This may seem minor, but it can actually make the difference as to whether or not your resume catches its viewer's attention, and subsequently gets read. Recently, I conducted an experiment by photocopying a number of off-white resumes onto white copy paper, and then shuffled them all together. I then asked several actors to examine the resumes in the pile. In every case, the resumes on off-white paper held the attention of the reader up to four times as long as those printed on white copy paper. All actors now own or have access to a personal computer, which makes the process of creating and printing a resume easier than in the past. Remember, your resume is half your calling card, so appearances are important. Any actor can and should have a nice-looking resume—even if it means cutting down on your beer supply for a week.

When laying out the resume, use larger, bold typeface for your name, which should be centered near the top of the page (see Appendices A and B). Centered directly below your name, in smaller print, place your union affiliations. If you don't have any union affiliations yet, don't worry about it. In time, you will. (Much more on that subject in the next chapter.) On the left side of the page, below your name and union affiliations, print your answering service and/or your telephone number. List your email address as well. Directly across from your telephone number, on the right side of the page, list your vital statistics: height, weight, hair color, and eye color. There is no need to list your age or age range, for a couple of reasons. First, your photo—if it looks just like you—will tell its viewer what to *perceive* your age range to be. This is another area of subjectivity. Second, actors, especially those with backgrounds in the theater, tend to give themselves an age range far wider than will be assessed by industry professionals. Usually, an agent or casting director will assess an actor's age range at an *approximate* span of five years, as in 25–30, 35–40, or even "late twenties to early thirties." The younger the actor, usually the narrower the assessment of the age range, as in 16–18, 18–21, or even 18–22, etc. Later in life, we are more likely to hear a wider range, such as 50–60 or 60–70, etc. Also, actors frequently give away their real age, which is not necessary or desirable, when they list their range. For example, when an actor lists a range of 30–40, guess how old she probably really is? Not 30!

For the New York actor, it is most often appropriate to list your theater credits first, followed by those of film, television, commercials, industrials, then training and special skills (see Appendix A). There will be exceptions to this format, of course. For example, if you landed a principal role in a feature-length film right after graduating from acting school, you would be more likely, of course, to start your resume with the category "Film" rather than "Theater"—which may consist solely of roles you played in school productions. The most impressive credits should hit the eye first. Logically then, Broadway credits first, followed by off-Broadway. If you have many areas of work such as national tours, regional theater, dinner theater, or summer stock, break your credits down into those subcategories for easy reading. For the New York actor whose credits consist only of off-off-Broadway, such as non-paying showcase and workshop productions, simply list the play, the role, and the theater, without a subcategory listing labeled "Off-off-Broadway" under the heading of "Theater." In a case such as this, you have the option of starting your resume with the listing "New York Theater." I suggest this, because "Off-off-Broadway" as a category at the very top of an actor's credentials sends a loud and immediate message to its reader: "No Broadway credits! No off-Broadway credits either!" There is nothing wrong with this, but from a marketing standpoint, there is certainly no need to call attention to it. If your only theater credits thus far are in amateur theater, or perhaps school productions, so be it. In the case of community theater, name the *theater* where the productions you were in were presented, as in "Johnston Lake Playhouse," rather than the more amateurish-sounding, "Johnson Community Players."

Remember, no one was born with impressive credits. If you work hard, things will change, and you will be replacing the old credits with new ones.

In Los Angeles, where the emphasis is on film and television, the preferred format lists *film* credits first, followed by *television,* and then *theater,* followed by *training* and *special skills* (see Appendix B). For the actor on either coast who has performed principal roles in film or television, be sure to list it as such—in parentheses—next to the character's name, as in: Joe (lead), or Adam (featured). Names of well-known directors should also be listed in all areas—film, television, and theater—on either coast. If you have played a principal role in a daytime television series, be sure to list it as such, as in Anne Evans (principal). If you have played Anne several times, be sure to list it as: Anne Evans (recurring). Of course, if Anne Evans was a contract role, you would list it accordingly: Anne Evans (contract role).

In the *commercials* category, it has been standard for decades for the actor to state: "Conflicts upon request" under the *commercials* heading. The reasoning is that if the actor lists the actual names of the products she has advertised, a casting director might assume that the actor is *currently* pitching a product which may be in conflict with a competitive product in the commercial now being cast. The actor would, of course, be ruled out of the running for the job, when in fact, the "competing" commercial may no longer be on the air, or the product's advertiser is no longer paying her a "holding fee" not to work for a competitor. However, it seems that almost every actor who has *never* done a television commercial has included a *commercials* category with the generic "conflicts upon request" printed alongside. Therefore, the actor who has actually done television commercials ends up with the same listing as the actor who has never done any, doing herself a disservice. For this actor, I suggest wording such as "On-camera principals for national network usage (tape upon request)" under the commercials category. If an actor is looking for representation, or perhaps *new* representation in commercials, this wording specifically tells its reader that the actor has already worked in this area of the industry. This is often a major concern, especially to larger talent agencies that represent actors exclusively for commercials. Such agencies are often looking for actors who already have a track record of "booking" commercials. Therefore, an actor who has done so sells herself short by approaching these agencies with the now virtually meaningless "Conflicts upon request." For the actor who has found work in *industrials,* which includes corporate videos and educational films, as well as live performances promoting a company, product, or service, I suggest a listing such as: "Live and on-camera for various corporations, including IBM and Xerox, Inc. (demo upon request)."

The *training* category is second to last on the resume, but do not underestimate its importance. Agents, casting directors, and directors will look for it, especially when they see that actual performing experience is minimal. Many use this as the "barometer of seriousness" of the newcomer, and many an actor has been granted an interview or audition on the basis of training alone. For the actor just starting out, being in a good acting class is essential, and the decision with whom to study is a personal one. Not unlike the search for a good photographer, looking for a good acting teacher involves talking with friends whose opinions you trust, looking through trade papers, and arranging to meet with or audit the classes of teachers who have been recommended to you, or whom you wish to investigate. Most importantly, choose the teacher you feel can best address your present needs in your development as an actor. Regardless of an acting teacher's reputation, if you do not like the way she deals with you or her manner of dealing with actors in general, then keep looking—few talent representatives have any interest in working with an actor who is not developing her craft through solid, ongoing training.

The final category, *special skills,* lists miscellaneous *strong* skills, ideally in this order: foreign languages in which you are fluent; dialects in which you are proficient; theatrical performance skills such as stage combat, mime, fencing, etc.; then musical instruments played. Last on the list should be sports that you play well, specific athletic skills, and any other skills that you feel are pertinent to your career as an actor. Never list anything you don't do *well* here—special skills means just that. This category is often a bizarre potpourri of activities in which the actor engages—I think I have seen everything imaginable on resumes over the years. Far be it from me to rule out that which some may consider a special skill, but such dubious gifts as "burping" (charming!), and "sleeping late" (industrious!), are probably better left unsaid.

DEMOS, DISCS, AND WEBSITES

Your very best film, television, and commercial work should be compiled and edited and placed on a disc. In days past, actors often had one "demo" (videotape cassette) for film and television work, and a separate demo for television commercials. Newer technology now allows the actor to have one on-camera demo—simply by separating the film/television work and the on-camera commercial spots into two different "chapters."

Your film and television chapter should not exceed five minutes and your commercial chapter should not exceed three to three and one-half minutes. Be sure to edit your selections in a way that shows your versatility and at the same time keeps the pace moving.

For the actor who has worked in voice-overs, an audio demo is an indispensable tool of the trade. The audio demo should also be in disc form and run under two minutes. Like your on-camera demo, your audio spots should be well-paced and selected to show your strength and versatility. Include spots that demonstrate a "range within your range," as voice-over artists and industry experts often put it, which means a demonstration of versatility that doesn't push the actor into trying to do too much in a short time.

Increasingly, actors are building websites as a means of "storage" for their headshots, resumes, and on-camera and voice-over demos, or "clips," as they are often called. In doing so, an interested industry person can download an actor's "arsenal" without the delay of a postal mailing or drop-off. Actors also often subscribe to various casting services that post an actor's photo, resume and clips for the availability of industry personnel. The most currently popular of these Internet casting services is Actors Access (actorsaccess.com), which allows actors who are subscribers to store a photo/resume and demo (optional). Subscribers are apprised—via email—of those roles being cast that are pertinent to the specific and personalized profile that the actor has filled out. Although Actors Access is owned by Breakdown Services, *most* of the projects being cast through Actors Access submissions are *not* the higher-level projects (i.e., *major* film, prime-time television, and stage productions) that are transmitted to talent representatives through Breakdown Services' original service, which is legally available only to agents and managers (more about this in Chapter 10).

YouTube (youtube.com) also allows actors to store clips or

demos of their work for viewing by the industry (or anyone else who would like to see it). If an actor has a demo placed on YouTube, he will typically put the link to the demo on his resume below his name and union affiliations (if any). As anyone can place virtually anything on YouTube, it's important to be aware that the venue or entity from which the demo comes will influence its credibility. For example, a quality scene from a top-rated network television show will make a far greater impression than a similar scene from an obscure independent film that never got distribution. From a legal standpoint, the placing of scenes on the Internet requires the approval of the project's production company, which will also apprise you of any copyright restrictions that may apply. Wonderful as this technology is, one should remember that an industry person often needs to be enticed into viewing or accessing any online materials that may be available about an actor.

In future chapters, I will discuss other Internet resources and what I consider to be the best uses of them, as well as outline various business communication techniques that can make industry persons want to learn more about you, thereby increasing the chances of viewing any online materials you may have. Ultimately, of course, your goal is for your materials and communication skills to lead to being called in—live and in person—for an interview or audition. But for now, let's talk a bit about the unions.

3

About the Unions

It is not my intention to minimize the importance of the talent unions in any way whatsoever. Unions and their members have fought—and continue to fight—long and hard to see that members are fairly compensated, and employed under acceptable working conditions. In time, you will want to become a member of the unions! However, I must point out that membership in the unions, or lack thereof, is often one of the most overrated concerns in the minds of beginning actors.

Lack of union membership in any of the three major unions—the American Federation of Television and Radio Artists (AFTRA), Actors' Equity Association (AEA), and the Screen Actors Guild (SAG)—should never keep one from pursuing work as an actor in a job under the jurisdiction of the unions. Of the three major unions, only SAG requires that a producer or advertising agency obtain "permission" to hire a performer who is not yet a union member. This permission is easily obtained, however. A SAG signatory producer or advertising agency fills out a simple form, and the actor is "waivered." By virtue of the Taft-Hartley Law, if you are the actor they want for the role, they can—and will—get the "waiver." SAG grants such waivers each and every day. Once "waivered," the actor is welcome to join SAG. Casting personnel are looking for the right actor for the role. This is how most actors become members of a performer's union in the first place.

I learned this lesson early and well the first week after I had moved to New York. Because I was not yet a member of Actors' Equity, I mistakenly thought that I could not submit my photo and resume to the office of the casting director of an upcoming off-Broadway production. My more professionally experienced roommate said, "Neither the casting director, the director, nor the producer of that play care whether you are a member of the union or not. If you are the one they want for the role, you will be hired. Then you will be issued a union contract. Then you will join the union. It's as simple as that."

He was right, and I never forgot it. Later, as a talent representative, I would secure literally thousands of auditions for actors in all areas of the industry—theater, film, television, commercials, and radio. *At no time was an audition ever contingent upon union membership.* Not once. This is not to say that casting directors will see anyone and everyone who is submitted to them by an agent. *Far from it.* Agents are not in the position of power that actors often perceive them to be. Casting directors often require a professional rundown of sorts before agreeing to set up an interview or audition for an actor. Depending upon the specifics of the project being cast, a casting director may find it necessary to "pass" on an actor whose credentials are minimal. From a casting director's point of view, professional experience, or the lack of it, can be a very valid reason to see, or not see, an actor for a given role. By virtue of the fact that an actor's credits are "light," it may also be the case that he is not a union member. By the same token, if an actor has impressive credentials, he will almost certainly be a member of at least one union. My point is that the actual issue of union membership *itself* is rarely, if ever, raised.

Recently, I called upon Jane Kronick, founder and former owner of New York's largest talent agency for young actors. I asked Jane if she had ever encountered union membership as a factor in a client's being granted an audition. Jane's response? "Never!" When asked if West Coast casting directors had ever asked about the union credentials of her clients, talent agent Holly Lebed—who had just returned from spending pilot season in Los Angeles—replied, "No, never." Logic dictates that if union membership is of little concern to a casting director, it is probably of little concern to agents. Other than by making a direct association with their clients' performing credits (e.g., a Broadway credit equals Equity membership), many agents could not even tell you offhand to which unions their clients belong.

Where, then, does this potentially harmful overemphasis on union membership come from? A couple of places. First, agents and casting personnel sometimes give it to actors as an excuse for their lack of interest. The actor often interprets this excuse as a *reason,* passes it along to other actors, and the myth proliferates. "Come back when you are in the unions, and I'll be able to do something for you," an actor may be told by an agent or casting director. Upon return a year later, union cards in tow, the actor will probably now be turned away for another "reason," unless the source of those union cards, i.e., the *work* that resulted in attaining union membership is, in itself, *impressive.*

I was once the recipient of this kind of excuse disguised as a reason. I was told by the director of a mini-series that someone else would have to be cast in a role for which I had auditioned, because, unfortunately, I was not a member of SAG. I quickly pointed out an oversight—that I was a member of SAG. Did this correction change things? Of course not! And if union membership had been a contingent factor in casting, why had I been auditioned in the first place if they thought I wasn't in the union? Because, as my roommate had taught me a few years earlier, it didn't matter. It is often easier to give someone an excuse than to give them a reason. (Later I met the actor who had been cast in "my" role. He said he was very happy to get the part, because now, at last, he could get his SAG card!) I knew the real reason why I hadn't gotten the part: I had given a less than spectacular reading at the call-back. Now this is what I call a *reason!*

Confusion over lack of union membership also emanates, at least in part, from the unions themselves. In the years past, Actors' Equity Association pressured theatrical producers to see Equity members for new productions by means of a procedure known as the Equity Principal Interview, commonly called the "EPI." After waiting, often for hours, a paid-up member of Equity was granted an "interview" with someone who he hoped had something to do with the casting of an upcoming production, which may or may not have already been cast. Since EPIs were open to Equity members only, non-union actors often mistakenly made the general assumption that producers, directors, and casting directors had no interest in actors who were not already members of the union. Not so. Producers, directors, and casting directors were and still are interested in genuine talent without respect to union membership. The EPIs had been instituted by Actors' Equity to serve its membership. Understandable as this was, non-union actors confused the dictate, and mistakenly assumed that it had come from the producers themselves. The myth set in.

Eventually, Equity replaced most of its Equity Principal Interviews (EPIs) with Equity Principal *Auditions* (EPAs), whereby Actors' Equity members were now allowed to perform a monologue or a song—depending upon the nature of the production or productions being cast. Performing, rather than being interviewed—which is where some of our finest performing artists fall short—served both the performer and those who hire the performer in far better fashion. Therefore, more actors—as well as singers and dancers—were cast from these Equity auditions than had previously benefited from the Equity "interview" system.

In 1988, Equity implemented a system called the Eligible Performers' Auditions. Although the initials (EPAs) remained the same, Equity allowed all performers who had attained specified earnings—or specified experience—as performers to audition for Equity productions without being a member of the union.

Equity has now reverted to its "Equity members only" audition system, however, resulting in many non-Equity actors wishing to become members of Equity in order to continue to attend these auditions. Although I generally recommend joining a union only when one is required to do so, one can become a member of the unions without being offered a contract as a principal performer. How does one become eligible to join the unions short of being offered such a contract? Here are the requirements.

AMERICAN FEDERATION OF TELEVISION AND RADIO ARTISTS (AFTRA)
www.aftra.com

The American Federation of Television and Radio Artists (AFTRA) has jurisdiction over radio, *videotaped* television (soap operas, variety shows, talk shows), and news programs, videotaped commercials, and industrials. AFTRA has an open-door policy. Make an appointment with the membership department of an AFTRA office, fork over the hefty initiation fee, plus dues for the first six months, and you're in. Simple as that. By virtue of the Taft-Hartley Law, an actor can work under the auspices of AFTRA for up to thirty days without joining the union. After the initial thirty-day period, the actor becomes a "must join" in the eyes of AFTRA, and indeed, "must join" before working again.

SCREEN ACTORS GUILD (SAG)
www.sag.com

Once the actor has been a member of AFTRA for one year, *and* has had a speaking part of any length under AFTRA's jurisdiction, he is then able to join SAG, if he chooses. Screen Actors Guild (SAG) has jurisdiction over most feature-length and theatrically released films, as well as *filmed* prime-time television, *filmed* commercials (that is, most television commercials), as well as *filmed* industrials.

An actor who has been a member of Actors' Equity for one year *and* has performed a principal role within Equity's jurisdiction is also eligible to join SAG if he chooses.

ACTORS' EQUITY ASSOCIATION (AEA)
www.actorsequity.org

Actors' Equity Association (AEA) has jurisdiction over Broadway, off-Broadway, League of Resident (LORT) Theaters, various other "legitimate" theaters, as well as industrials that are performed live. An actor is eligible to join Actors' Equity Association after being a member of either AFTRA or SAG for one year and having performed a principal role within that union's jurisdiction. One can also become a member of Equity through the Equity Membership Candidate Program (EMC), which entails working for fifty weeks (forty if one passes a written test) at participating Equity theaters. In a recent development, Equity now allows a one-year member of AFTRA or SAG who has worked for three days as an extra within that union's jurisdiction to join Equity.

As I mentioned earlier, it is my belief—generally speaking—that an actor should join a union when membership becomes necessary, although many actors who have built a solid body of stage work—albeit non-union—decide to join Equity in the above manner in order to attend Equity auditions in hopes of advancing their career levels. Although the myth persists that actors are not cast from these auditions, this is a false and destructive notion circulated with alarming regularity by actors. Realistically, however, the "level" of the stage project being cast (i.e., Broadway, off-Broadway vs. regional, stock, etc.) and the size of the cast, along with the status quo of an actor's resume, are all factors in whether or not an actor is likely to be cast from an EPA.

In addition to the primary purpose of attending Equity-sponsored auditions—to secure employment—there are ancillary benefits as well. These auditions are one way for the unrepresented actor to build up a roster of casting directors who know him, a major concern of agents—as we shall see in Chapter 6. As we shall also see in great detail, high-level call-backs are amongst the most powerful progress that one can report to both agents and casting directors. All three benefits await those who perform well at these auditions. Remember, however, that once an actor becomes a member of Equity, he is precluded from appearing in non-Equity productions, and is also now competing with actors at a higher career level than before. Therefore, the decision to join Equity without benefit of an Equity contract (at which point one would be required to join) is a decision one should not make lightly. Eventually, however, membership in at least one union will become necessary *and desirable* for the professional working actor on either coast. In the next chapter, Television: Daytime vs. Prime Time, we will discover ways to get acting work, and qualify to become a member of the unions as well.

4

Television: Daytime vs. Prime Time

There are, of course, many areas of the entertainment industry—union and non-union—that offer gainful employment to actors.

For the professional newcomer, working in daytime television is one of the best ways to become eligible to join all the unions—and often pay membership fees with earnings made from one's work as an actor.

At the time of this writing there are seven soaps on the air—five days a week, thirty-five episodes in all—which provide employment opportunities for thousands of actors each year.

The pursuit of soap opera work is more common in New York than in Los Angeles, however, for a few reasons. Although there are now several prime-time series shot in New York, the majority of dramatic television airtime emanating out of New York—on a day-to-day basis—is still comprised of soaps. In terms of salaries at least, soap opera contract roles are amongst the "best" acting jobs in New York. In addition, many New York actors who do a soap by day are found working in the theater, which is often their first love, at night. Although a formidable workload for any actor, this double-duty is not uncommon. In doing so, the actor keeps flexing her acting muscles, while staying visible to the theatrical community, as well as the film and prime-time television industries, which often overlook the soap world in their own casting processes. Many New York "soap" actors who went on to film and prime-time television success managed to do so, at least in part, by appearing in plays either on Broadway or off, while working in daytime television. Among them are: Kathleen Turner, Kevin Kline, Kevin Bacon, Christopher Walken, and Sigourney Weaver, to name a very small handful.

In Los Angeles, home to the bulk of the television industry, soaps are not the most desirable work in television. Compared to prime-time television salaries, the earnings in daytime television can be relatively modest. And while the New York actor might work on or off-Broadway during a long-term soap stint, the Los Angeles soap actor does not have this same option. Less often do we see a Los Angeles soap actor "make the jump" to film or prime-time television in a very big way. There are exceptions, of course, but they are not as common—especially in comparison to the number of New York actors who have made this same leap. If you look into the careers of the many film and prime-time television stars who have a daytime soap in their "past," you will discover that in most cases it is a *New York* soap. Often the New York actor's exposure in the theater enabled them to make this leap. At the same time, the old stigma of being branded as a "soap opera actor" no longer exists, and actors are crossing media with greater frequency than before.

East coast and west, work on soap operas breaks down into the following categories: contract roles, non-contract recurring roles, day player roles, under-fives, and extras.

Contract roles are the roles that are played by the soaps' stars, as well as most of the regular cast.

Non-contract recurring roles are principal roles that are played by actors who appear from time to time, or even on a fairly regular basis. The major difference between the actor who has a contract and the recurring non-contract principal player is a little matter known as the *guarantee.* The contract player is guaranteed a certain—and negotiable—number of appearances each week; even if she doesn't appear, she must be paid her "guarantee." The disadvantage is that, unlike the non-contract recurring principal, the contract player cannot quit the soap job until her contract is up. The non-contract player, however, is free to accept other jobs that may necessitate her leaving the soap.

Although the overwhelming majority of "regulars" are on contract, there is no absolute way of knowing for sure who is and who is not. Sometimes even a rather high-profile, prominently featured player is not being held under contract.

The *day player* is a principal who usually appears for—you guessed it—one day. If the day player role keeps popping up, it then becomes—you guessed it again—a non-contract recurring role. If the non-contract recurring role becomes essential to the story line, the actor playing the role may be asked to sign a contract.

The *under-five* is a role for which the actor has literally under five lines to speak. The *extra,* of course, has no lines.

Contract roles are the highest-paying work that soaps have to offer. Unfortunately, however, there are not really as many of these kinds of roles available as many would hope. In addition, the older the character of the contract role being cast, the more likely it will go to an actor who already has a proven track record in the world of daytime television. Since new contract roles on soaps tend to be on the young side, "older" can even mean a character in her late twenties or early thirties. The older the character, the more likely this is to be the case. Often, a role for a character in her forties or fifties will go to an actor who has had a high-profile career in film, prime-time television, or in the theater—and is not currently in demand in those areas of the industry.

The biggest "turnover" market in contract roles is for the young and the beautiful (the bold and the restless?). As I mentioned in Chapter 1, often a contract role will go to a young actor who has the requisite physical attributes, but little professional experience.

The casting of the contract role is, at least from the representative's standpoint, a fairly simple process. In most cases, a role description is sent out by the show's casting director to Breakdown Services for the agents to see. Agents submit photos and resumes from which the casting director sets up audition appointments. From that initial group, some will be called back for a subsequent audition that will be viewed by the soap's producer. From these call-backs will be chosen those actors who are to be screen-tested. Before the actual screen-tests, negotiable offers go out to these actors' agents. Once the monies and guarantees have been agreed upon, the offer is drawn up. This is called the "pre-test deal." In essence, it is the actor's contract. It must be signed by the actor, and guarantees the soap executives and the network that upon being offered the role, the actor will indeed accept it. The screen-tests are then viewed by the soap executives and the network, a decision is made, and an actor who has just been through a very nerve-racking process has a job.

While contract roles may elude the less spectacularly resplendent actor, there is still a volume of work available each week for the truly presentable looking.

What are the advantages to seeking work on soap operas? First, the facts. As I mentioned in Chapter 3, a performer may work under AFTRA's jurisdiction (which covers soaps) for up to thirty days before membership becomes mandatory. That is, one can make some money working under the union's jurisdiction before paying the membership fee and the first set of dues.

Remember, too, that an actor need only utter so much as one word of dialogue, that is, an "under-five," and after being a member of AFTRA for one year, the actor is then automatically eligible to join SAG *if* she chooses. Or after having been a member of AFTRA for one year and having had an under-five *or* having worked three days as an extra, one is also able to join Actors' Equity, *if* one chooses.

One actor who came to see me, and was new to the business of acting, got very lucky right away. She was given three weeks of work as an extra in a soap opera courtroom scene. In the course of this three-week period of employment, she a) got a professional credit for her resume; b) made more than enough money to join AFTRA; c) put some money in the bank; and d) knew that having worked at least three days as an extra in a production under AFTRA's jurisdiction would qualify her for membership in Equity *if she so chose*—one year after joining AFTRA.

On the other side of the spectrum, another actor who came to see me took a *year* before he got work on a soap. But after he did, he got at least one job per month, and by the end of the year, wound up in essentially the same position as the actor in story number one. It just took longer.

My own experience in daytime television was closer to example two. My first professional acting job was as an extra on *Guiding Light*. In time, I was "promoted" to speaking roles.

This brings us to an age-old question concerning soap opera extra work. Does it hurt one's chances of becoming a contract player? After nearly three decades of being involved with the world of New York daytime television, these are my observations on the subject. Doing *some* work as an extra on soaps will probably never damage an actor's chances of becoming a contract player. Of the many young soap opera contract players I represented, there was not one who did *not* have some previous history of having worked as a soap opera extra. I'm not saying that they made an active pursuit of this kind of work, only that somewhere along the line it came their way, they did it, and it never kept them from being considered for a contract role. One young actor I know was working as an extra on a soap when the show's head casting director spotted him and called him aside to discuss a new contract role, for which he was subsequently auditioned and screen-tested. There were many young extras on the set that day—why was he singled out? Looks. Herein, I think, lies a large part of the answer to the soap opera extra work issue. *Most* of the actors working as extras on soap operas do not have the physical requisites to become contract players. This is not to say that extras on soaps are not physically attractive. They very often are. As I pointed out, a few will become contract players. Yet, if you were to look closely at a soap opera restaurant scene, for example, you would see that the actors at the "surrounding" tables don't usually look quite like the principals at the center table. At these surrounding tables, we sometimes see spectacles, receding hairlines, and even, God help us, the occasional bald spot. Eyeglasses, receding hairlines, and bald spots are not regularly seen on young actors in the foreground on soap operas. On occasion, I have seen an especially stunning "extra" seated at a surrounding table eventually rise and join those at the center table, only to confirm my suspicions. A table-hopping contract player!

Frequently, an actor will erroneously believe she has been stigmatized by her work as an extra. Often, however, it is a case of the very common syndrome of an actor not seeing herself clearly. An example: Recently, in discussing the soap opera extra issue, an actor told me that another actor said he knew "for a fact" that he was not read for a new contract role on a specific soap because he had worked regularly on that show as an extra. He had managed to get an audition for the role, and when he arrived at the audition, the casting director looked at him and said, "Oh, it's you! We know you well! There's no need to read for us!" He assumed he got bagged because of the extra stigma. I asked the actor who told me this tale how the second actor had gotten the audition in the first place. "From his photo," he replied. Just as I suspected. I said, "If the casting director did not recognize him from his photo, and only recognized him upon his arrival in person, then this actor does not resemble his photograph." The actor who told me the story said, "You're right! I saw his photo. He was extremely handsome in the picture, but in person, he was only about average looking." This is a more likely reason this actor did not get to read for the contract role. I am convinced that any actor who is "right" by the standards of daytime television will get a chance to read for soap opera contract roles. While soaps are willing to meet pretty people, an actor who auditions poorly at a particular soap opera may not find it easy to gain entry to that same office when they are casting another role, however.

Soap opera casting directors frequently call in actors from the actor's mailings to read for these roles *if* their look is right. Yet most young actors who *genuinely* possess the look that daytime television seeks will, unless they are totally devoid of ability or ambition, before long probably find someone to represent them for work in this area of the industry. I think it's as simple as that.

With respect to the issue of extra work—in general—we must consider something else. If an actor is talented and committed, we can assume that some area of her career will start to move. At some point, she will then put extra work behind her, if, in fact, she is doing it at all. Yet, there are times in the course of many actors' careers when working as an extra may be necessary, either to meet the required earnings to have the union pay their health insurance, or purely out of financial need.

In soap operas, there simply are not enough contract roles that need to be cast to accommodate anywhere near the number of actors who could fill them. One young actor I represented got screen-tested for every role in his age range for every soap on the air for a period of over six years before he landed a contract. Longer than most, to be sure, but it is not uncommon for an actor to get as far as the screen-test for at least a few soaps over a period of a couple of years, before actually hitting. By virtue of their infrequency and specific requirements, contract roles on soaps do not let one "get up to bat" often enough to make this area of the industry a realistic goal for most actors.

Contract roles aside, however, there is a large amount of work available on soaps. Thousands of actors have several soap credits on their resume, credits that they acquired through their own efforts—that is, without the help of representation. I worked regularly on almost all New York soaps at a time when there were ten in New York City alone. I have passed my method for getting work along to many other actors who have experienced similar results. By implementing this strategy, actors have gotten work as extras, under-fives, day players, recurring roles, and in a few cases, even contract roles.

The greatest amount of available work on soap operas falls into the categories of extras and under-fives. If you feel that you are contract role "material," and believe that the ongoing pursuit of what may turn out to be minor work on soaps will harm your chances of being considered for a contract—and I acknowledge that many believe that—you have two options. Either approach only two or three of the soaps on the coast where you live, instead of all four or five—or put your efforts into finding representation, instead of approaching the soaps on your own behalf. For those who are interested in pursuing soap work on their own, this procedure will take all of about fifteen minutes each week, and the results can be extremely gratifying. Here goes.

On the first week, send a photo, resume, and typed cover letter to all the assistant or associate casting directors of soap operas as listed in *Call Sheet,* formerly *Ross Reports* (see Appendix E). *Call Sheet* lists New York and Los Angeles talent agencies, independent casting companies, as well as casting personnel at prime-time television series and soap operas. If you live in New York, contact only the New York soaps. If you live in L.A., contact only the L.A. soaps. It is of utmost importance to include a cover letter with *every* photo and resume sent out (not just for soaps).

Although the hallmark of a good cover letter is *brevity,* its purpose is not only to explain why the photo is being sent, but to include, or emphasize information that may increase your chances of getting an interview or audition. If your training is your strongest suit thus far, open with that. Your soap cover letter might go something like this:

> Dear [*Name* of Assistant or Associate Casting Director]: (Very Important!)
> I have recently graduated from The Neighborhood Playhouse here in New York. Since graduating, I have appeared in lead roles in two independent short films, and am eager to do more on-camera acting. I would very much like to work on *All My Children* and would appreciate the opportunity to meet with you. To view a demo of my work, please visit [list your website], or you may also see it on YouTube at [list link].
> Thank you.
> Sincerely,
> Brian O'Neil

On subsequent weeks, send a *photo postcard* to each soap assistant or associate casting director. The message should follow a format *similar* to this:

> Dear [*Name* of Assistant/Associate Casting Director]:
> Recently sent my photo and resume to you. Since then, I have [*Brief Progress Report*]. Hope to meet with you soon.
> Thank you.
> Sincerely,
> Brian O'Neil

What constitutes a brief progress report? Anything in the following categories:

- Any acting work you got, paying or non-paying.
- Any acting work you *almost* got—call-backs for paying or

nonpaying work. Call-backs mean you are auditioning well and being taken seriously by those who cast. Call-backs make good progress reports. There will be much more on the power of call-backs in the coming chapters!

• Any promising meeting with agents. As in: "Met with Joe Smith at Artists Unlimited. We're going to start working together. Hope to hear from you soon. Thank you," etc.

Successful meetings with agents help to establish credibility in the mind of casting personnel. When activity is slower for you than you might like, and you still wish to "stay in touch" *and* show progress, you can always report a variation on "old" news, as in: "Have been auditioning for commercials through Joe Smith at Artists Unlimited. Would like to meet with you. Thank you," etc.

These are just a few ideas, but showing progress is always the important factor. And, of course, it must be true! Also, it is more valuable from a self-marketing standpoint to say: "I would like to work for you," or "I would like to audition for you," than to say, "I am available for extra work." By virtue of the fact that you are contacting them on a weekly basis, they will know that you are "available." More importantly, by asking for "extra" work, you are saying, "I'd like some work with no lines, please." As I pointed out, most of the available work is in the area of extras and under-fives, and will probably be what you will be offered. However, as I also mentioned, actors are called in for all-size roles from this manner of self-submission, so why market yourself in this limiting way? Get in the habit of presenting yourself for best results. I have often seen postcards from extremely attractive actors repeatedly requesting "extra" work. Why are they going out of their way to mention that they are seeking non-speaking roles? By the same token, if you are an actor who no longer does extra work, but would like to work on soaps, be sure to let the casting personnel know this. Each time you write, say: "Am seeking work as an under-five or principal only." This will cut down on the amount of work for which you may be called, but at least you've told them what you will and will not do, and therefore will not waste their time or annoy them by calling you for work that you will not accept.

If you were to do a day's work as an extra in a film, commercial, or industrial, and you reported it to a soap opera casting director, it would be better to write: "Just did a day's work on the new Hal Smith film, *Heaven's Above.* Would like to work for you too," than to say, "Just worked as an extra on the new Hal Smith film, *Heaven's Above.* Am available for soap extra work too."

So, then, the gist of this is to report progress—briefly—each week, if possible. Soaps get *thousands* of pieces of mail each week and, to be realistic, it may take some time before your face and messages start to "kick in." If you are cast in a quality theater production, be sure to send a flyer or invitation to the soap casting personnel. (In Chapter 7, I will discuss strategies for creating theater audition opportunities.)

"Suppose a few weeks go by, and I have nothing new to report?" actors will sometimes ask me. If that is the case two things are possible. Either you are not out there auditioning or creating audition opportunities as often as you should be, or you are not auditioning well enough to be getting called back. Either situation warrants examination. More on that in the next chapter! Ideally, the actor who wants to work on soaps should be contacting them every week, or every second week, until she hears from them. How long does this take? It depends upon the specific needs of the individual soaps, your age range and overall appearance, and, of course, the content of your messages. Some actors get called quite quickly. My own method was, as you have probably guessed, to write each week, telling them something new with each writing. I decided that if I heard from no one after seven months, I would be confident that they would know who I was, and I would telephone them and ask for an appointment—which is what I did. Although soap opera casting directors understandably discourage actors from telephoning their offices, I felt at that point I had *earned* the right to telephone. I got my first appointment and subsequently my first job on my very first call. Another office told me to "check in by mail," which I did for three more months and then called again. This time they saw me. My second job (*All My Children*)! As I mentioned, eventually almost every show came through. Once in the door, I worked repeatedly for everybody, eventually joined all the unions, and made some nice income besides.

To repeat, it is of utmost importance to be building credibility with the brief message on your photo postcard. Those who hire like to hire those whom others also hire. As you build credibility, and continue to persist, those who do the casting are more likely to accept a telephone call from you, if they don't call you first.

Example: On the day I opened Acting as a Business, my career-planning and consulting service for actors, my very first client told me that he was interested in pursuing work on soap operas. Recalling how I had done it, I started to tell him what I thought he should do. "But I *have* been writing to them each week since January," Greg told me. This was now September. "Well, what do you say each week?" I asked. "That I am available for extras and under-fives," came the deadly response. "Is that all?" I asked. "That's it," he said. "That's what you've been telling them for thirty-five weeks?" I said. "Greg, you've told them nothing! You've been sticking your hand out for thirty-five weeks. You're out there getting work in commercials and industrials, tell them about that. Try it my way from now until the end of the year. On January second of next year, *call* them up and ask for an appointment. You might get a voice-mail, but call. You will, by then, have written to each of them fifty-two times. I guarantee you that they will all know who you are. You hereby have my permission to call!"

I heard from Greg again on January third. He had followed my instructions to the letter. On January second, he had made his calls. He got two appointments, followed by two jobs, one of which was a speaking role. I said to him, "You could have written to them weekly for the rest of your life, and never heard anything. But you paved your way in, and when you made your calls, you had earned your appointments. They knew that, and they gave you a break." Soon Greg was working on soaps frequently. In a short while he was in all the unions and working in all areas of the business. This kind of scenario unfolds daily, many times over, but usually to the actor who has "bugged" these people. Bugged them in a *good* way, I mean!

Actors sometimes ask me why I spend more time talking about soaps than I do about prime-time television, especially in today's market where the popularity of soaps has declined in the last decade or so. The answer, in a word, is *access*. Most actors who get a small speaking part on an episode of a prime-time show get the job through the help of an agent. Most actors who get a small speaking part on an episode of a soap get the job *without* the help of an agent. That is, they get it through their own efforts. Another reason I advocate working on soaps, as the earlier part of this chapter indicates, is to help the actor begin the process of *qualifying* to join *all* the unions—which is often easier to do through working under AFTRA's jurisdiction than through SAG's.

Here's why. First, let's start by taking a look at some union differences between working on television—even in the capacity of an "extra" under AFTRA's jurisdiction (videotaped daytime soaps), versus working as an "extra" under SAG's jurisdiction (filmed prime-time shows).

If one is hired as an "extra" on a television show (or film, for that matter) under SAG's jurisdiction, and one is *not* a member of SAG, her pay will be *lower* than that of the "extra" who is already a member of SAG, and who is working on the same show. Conversely, if an actor is hired as an "extra" on a show that is under AFTRA's jurisdiction (daytime soaps) and she is *not* a member of AFTRA, her pay will be the *same* as that of the "extra" who is already a member of AFTRA. In short, there is no "class distinction" of pay under AFTRA's jurisdiction, whether or not the "extra" is already a member of AFTRA. Not so with SAG.

Secondly, an "upgrade" (an "extra" suddenly being offered one or more lines right on the set due to unexpected script changes) happens on the set of a soap (AFTRA), regardless of the "extra's" union membership, *or lack of it.* Not so on the set of a SAG production. In the last chapter, I mentioned that a "waiver" is necessary for a non-SAG actor to be offered "lines" (or work as a principal under SAG's jurisdiction). And while the "waiver" is easy to obtain for most casting purposes, the urgency of the unexpected "upgrade" on the set does not allow time for the SAG "waiver" to be obtained. Therefore, the "upgrade" will be offered to an "extra" who is *already* a member of SAG.

Third, when an actor has started to work as an "extra" on a

soap, once thirty days have passed on the calendar, and the actor is offered work once again, she will be a "must join" and AFTRA membership will become mandatory. Not so with SAG, where a non-SAG actor can work indefinitely as an "extra" and not qualify to join SAG. As I mentioned on page 36, a one-year member of AFTRA who works as an "extra" for three days under AFTRA's jurisdiction is then qualified to join Actors' Equity Association. In addition, an actor who is a one-year member of AFTRA and performs an "under-five" is able to join SAG and/or Equity.

For all the above reasons then, I lean more toward advocating working as an "extra" under AFTRA's jurisdiction than under SAG's—for the actor who is not a union member.

Okay, by now I suspect you want to get away from all of this union talk and find out more about how to get an agent! So, onward we go to the next chapter.

5

———◆———

Approaching the Agents

A number of ways exist by which an actor may find himself invited into an agent's office. By far, the best way is to be asked in as a result of an agent's having seen your work. This means, quite simply, that this agent likes your work and is interested in the possibility of representing you. You are part, but by no means all, of the way home.

Another way is through the referral of a casting director who has taken an active interest in helping you find representation. A referral by an actor who is already represented by the agent can also be an effective door-opener, or you may be fortunate enough to be granted an interview on the basis of your photo, resume, and cover letter alone. Another method is through a photo, resume, and cover letter that have been *followed up* by ongoing correspondence that shows true career progress.

Before I elaborate on cover letters and the demonstration of career progress, let me explain why getting yourself in the door by having your work seen is the best means of entry. An interview granted as a result of a referral by a casting director or agency client may be the *easiest* way in the door, but the interview has been arranged based on someone *else's* relationship with the agent, someone *else's* relationship with you, and someone *else's* opinion of you. Agents must always maintain the favor of casting directors, as casting directors are the potential "buyers" of the agent's clients' services. Therefore, an agent will almost always agree to meet with an actor who has been referred by a casting director. And many agents—again as a courtesy gesture—will see an actor who has been referred to them by one of their clients. In both instances, neither the casting director, nor the agent's client, may be keenly aware of the agent's likes, dislikes, or specific needs. Therefore, the *desire* to meet the actor has not been inspired directly by the actor himself. In other words, such meetings are often granted out of obligation or as favors, not out of direct interest of the agent. None of this is to say that the actor should not take advantage of every contact and legitimate referral. I only mean to point out that I have seen many actors hold very high hopes about a meeting that has been arranged through a mutual party—only to have disappointing results.

Earlier, I mentioned that you may be granted an interview on the basis of your photo, resume, and cover letter alone. Let's assume you are new to the business of acting, with no legitimate contacts to exploit, and are starting the search for representation. Rather than telling the agent that you are "dedicated, committed, and talented, and would probably be an asset to the agency," as well as other "Says who?" qualities, let's follow a format similar to the one in the previous chapter. Again, we'll keep the emphasis on the more tangible—*the training*. Your typed cover letter might go something along the lines of the following:

Dear [Name of AGENT] (very important!):

I have recently graduated from The Neighborhood Playhouse here in New York City. Since graduating, I have appeared in two NYU student films. I'm now continuing my studies with Terry Schreiber.

At present, I am looking for representation in all areas, and would appreciate the opportunity to meet with you at your convenience.

Thank you for your interest.

Sincerely,

Brian O'Neil

As I mentioned in the last chapter, the purpose of a cover letter is not only to explain why the photo and resume are being sent, but to emphasize or include information that may increase your chances of getting an interview. You can put information in a cover letter that you *cannot* put on your resume. As I briefly mentioned with regard to the soap opera follow-up campaign, a report of one job—or more—that you *almost* got in the recent past can be highly effective. It is also a good way of getting *yourself* in the door.

Reporting the "almosts" comes as a surprise to most actors, probably because we are so often told that "almost doesn't count." In the business of acting, "almost" often counts for a lot. Let me give you an example of reporting an "almost" that had far-reaching results. Recently, a young actor, new to New York, came to see me.* She did not know which agents to approach, or how to contact them in an effective manner. I

---

* I retain this example from earlier editions of *Acting as a Business* as many actors have reported similar results with such productions as *Rent, Hairspray, The Lion King*, etc. The power of the high-level call-back will be a recurring theme throughout this book.

asked her for a rundown of her professional activities since she had been in New York. I learned that she had been attending every audition she could find that she felt had a role in it for which she might be suited. Good. I then asked her what kind of results she had been getting. She reported that one of the many auditions she had attended had brought her especially favorable response. She had attended an open call listed in *Back Stage* for "future replacements and understudies" for the role of Cosette, in the Broadway production of *Les Miserables*. She had been called back to audition two more times. While the final results had brought her little more than frustration when she was ultimately not cast, I demonstrated the potential value of the situation by suggesting that she send the following cover letter—along with her photo and resume—to a number of talent agents who represented actors for theater, film, and television, as listed in *Call Sheet:*

> Dear (Name of Agent):
>
> Enclosed is my photo and resume. Since moving to New York three months ago, I have auditioned three times—two of them call-backs—for the role of Cosette in the Broadway production of *Les Miserables* cast by Jamibeth Margolis.
>
> In addition, I have recently enrolled in scene study class with Michael Howard. I am now looking for representation, and would appreciate the opportunity to meet with you at your convenience.
>
> Thank you.
>
> Sincerely,
>
> Sandra A.

Sandra initially expressed some reluctance about starting her letter with what she felt was meaningless information—call-backs for a part she didn't get. I explained to her that an agent would interpret it as a way of saying that she was of Broadway caliber—since she had been called back twice for a major role.

Why would call-backs make such a statement? Well, first it's important to remember just how subjective the casting process is! Most likely, Sandra didn't get cast because whoever was making the decision decided that someone else was more suited for the role. There could be any number of reasons why Sandra was not ultimately selected—not the least of which could have been her lack of credits, or even that she bore a resemblance to someone-in-charge's ex-wife who had fleeced him for everything. She most likely wouldn't have gotten as far as she did in the casting process if she had been found lacking in talent.

Sandra reported to me several days later that she had sent her photo and resume to a few agents and had already had an interview with one of them. When I asked her the details of the meeting, she said that the agent had asked her right away about her audition for *Les Miserables,* and the subsequent call-backs. Good; the mention of these high-level (Broadway) call-backs had piqued the agent's interest. What happened next is equally, if not more, important.

The agent asked Sandra if she had been submitted for a new Broadway production that was about to be cast. Sandra replied that she had not, and the agent was free to suggest her to the casting director.* The agent then telephoned the casting director of the upcoming production, informed him that he had a suggestion for one of the roles, to which the casting director responded: "Tell me about her." This is a casting director's

---

* This process is called *clearing*. It is a necessary procedure for an agent who wants to submit freelance (that is, unsigned) talent for theater, film, and television projects. In essence, the actor is giving the agent "permission" to be his agent for that specific project.

polite way of urging an agent to give him information that may interest him enough to set up an interview or audition with the actor. "Well, you don't know her yet, but she was recently called back twice for Cosette in *Les Miserables* here on Broadway!" "In that case, I would like to see her Wednesday morning at eleven!" came the casting director's reply.

It should be clear by now just how effective that sentence in Sandra's cover letter was. It not only got her in the agent's door, it got her another audition with a second casting director. Most agents' submissions do *not* result in an audition. I am not suggesting that every agent will immediately get on the telephone with a casting director without benefit of seeing your work. However, a strong example of your potential can be indicated by the response you get from major casting directors. Sandra's track record was enough to establish credibility in the eyes of one agent and a second casting director. Casting directors compete with each other for jobs. They know each other's standards. Had she not mentioned these call-backs in her letter, she probably would not have gotten the interview with the agent, and the subsequent audition for the new Broadway production. Obviously, the higher the level of the job for which you got called back—Broadway, off-Broadway, regional theater, feature film, or television projects, for example—along with the number of call-backs and the name of the casting director, the stronger the impact. Unlike the soap opera "campaign"—where reporting all career progress including callbacks at every level can bring results—I suggest being more selective with progress that is reported to agents. Unlike the casting personnel at soaps, who actually *hire* actors, the agent *invests* in the actor. Agents work on speculation. *Therefore, I don't recommend reporting to agents call-backs on showcases, staged readings, and other non-paying projects.* Chances are the agent wasn't involved in submitting actors on these projects, which will probably render your progress report virtually meaningless. The stakes are not high enough. And certainly, such progress would have no place in a cover letter. Now there will be exceptions to this, as in a case where a prominent director or writer may seek submissions through agents for a project in its early stages. If you know this to be the case, then be sure to report any close calls.

So, then when you are reporting call-backs the results will most likely be better when the agents you are contacting have submitted clients for the projects in which you were almost cast. The following example illustrates a situation whereby an actor used call-backs in her *follow-up* campaign to get agency representation, and the results paid off almost immediately. The actor, Janet, told me she had done a "mass mailing" (a term that always makes me shudder—sounds too much like "mass murder") to all the agents in New York who represented actors for film, television, and theater, as listed in *Call Sheet*. Janet next attempted to contact these agents by telephone in hopes of being granted an interview. On the telephone she was told—in varying degrees of politeness—that if anyone at the agency was interested in meeting her, she would be contacted. (Sound familiar?) Janet was not contacted by any of the agents and did not know what to do next. I told her to do nothing where the agents were concerned, but to continue to audition with the resources she had. When she had some progress to report—even a call-back, or of course, a *production in which she was appearing to invite them to*—then, and not until then, should she contact these agents again.

When you are contacting an agent you have contacted by mail before—and are hoping to meet—ask yourself this: "Does what I am about to write show progress? Will it present me at a higher level of value than I was at the last time this person heard from me?" If not, unless you have a specific reason for writing, hold off until you have something to say. Unfortunately, many actors do not take full advantage of things that do show progress and report things that are virtually meaningless. Or, as many actors are quick to tell me, they contact agents, "only when I am working." This strategy does not allow an actor to take full advantage of all the times when one should and *must* make contact, for the simple reason that most actors are not working enough to begin with. Also, the actor then runs the risk of telling those he is contacting that he is not available for any projects currently being cast.

Several weeks after Janet's "mass mailing" she auditioned— through a referral—for a role in a comedy feature film. Although she was ultimately not cast, she auditioned very well and was called back to read for the director. That is when she again contacted the agents who had not responded to her "mass mailing" and telephone follow-up. She wrote the following message on the back of her photo postcards:

> Dear [Name of agent]:
> Sent my photo and resume to you several weeks ago. Just wanted to let you know that I recently got called back by Fairfax Casting for the role of Sally in *Welcome to Buzzsaw.* Still hope to meet with you!
> Sincerely,
> Janet B.

Janet told me that on the following day, one of the agents to whom she had sent a postcard telephoned her and told her that several of his clients, a few of whom were regularly working actors, had auditioned for the same role, none had been called back—and yes, indeed, he wanted to meet Janet right away. As this example illustrates, when you report callbacks to agents whose clients auditioned for the same role, the agent will compare the response you got to that his clients got, and your message will speak to the agent in a very real and meaningful way. If you persist by reporting your good responses in this way, you will find yourself being asked in for an interview by at least some of the agents you are contacting. Remember, they are thinking of you only when they are hearing from you, so it is critical that when they do hear from you, you tell them something that has some meaning for them. In terms of building credibility, call-backs are far more powerful than reporting a new class you've signed up for, that someone in your class said it's a great agency, or myriad other excuses to run your name and face by an agent you wish to meet.

Here's another reason why call-backs establish credibility. Agents live in a world of call-backs. Most of their best clients get called back a great deal, and then don't get the job. Most of the time. This continues until the client eventually lands a job, and, hopefully, becomes more and more in demand—a truly precious place for an actor to be. Call-backs are the means by which an agent monitors *response* to his clients. Frequently, call-backs can make the deciding difference as to whether or not an agent will hold on to a client. No one, not even the actor, knows better than an agent how long it can take for a client to land a really great job. It can take years for an agent's investment in a client—time, telephone calls from coast-to-coast, sending photos by costly messenger service, express-mailing of demo reels, etc., etc.—to really pay off. Many actors don't realize that it costs money to represent an actor. Call-backs, by their nature, are *promising*.

The key is to keep your correspondence ongoing for as long

as it takes you to get representation. Most actors take stabs. They write to an agent once, follow up with a phone call, send a postcard or maybe several that tell the agent virtually nothing, and then complain that they can't find an agent. Agents may need to hear from you not once or twice, but many times before your progress reports register strongly enough for them to call you.

"How will an agent know I am telling the truth when I am reporting call-backs?" is a question actors frequently ask me. The more specific you are with details, the more likely you are to be telling the truth. People who lie tend to be general. Besides, I don't know one actor who would write to agents on a regular basis, telling them about projects he was being called back for—including the name of the casting director, the role, and the number of call-backs—unless it was true. The information is too easy to verify. Recently, a young actor told me she had been writing to a number of agents on a weekly basis, telling them only, "I'd really like to meet with you" for ten straight weeks. When this method proved fruitless, on the eleventh week, she scrawled this fabricated addendum: "Been getting a lot of call-backs lately!" (Note the general "a lot of call-backs.") One of the agents to whom she had been writing had her in for an interview. When she innocently asked what it had been that finally made him decide to call her, he replied, "The call-backs! What have they been for?" Well, she had not known the power her lie would have, and she sat there red-faced and speechless. Don't lie. If you are not getting call-backs, examine why you aren't. Here's a look at some of the most common pitfalls in the audition experience.

First, look at the visuals. How do you present yourself? Do you dress appropriately? Recently, I met an actor who had just come from auditioning for Blanche in *A Streetcar Named*

Desire. She was wearing a very short, very tight mini-dress with black stockings and stiletto high-heels. For Blanche in *Streetcar*? No. For a Jennifer Lopez look-alike contest, maybe. I'm not suggesting that you go in costume, only that you wear what makes sense.

What about your audition material itself? Is it appropriate? A lot of actors gaffe in this department. Let's say you are auditioning for a theater company whose season includes classics by Ibsen, Shaw, and Chekhov, and contemporary plays by Mamet, Shepard, and Shanley. You are asked to bring two pieces, one classical and one contemporary. You have such pieces. Your classical piece is from Moliere, and you have a contemporary piece by Gurney. Classical and contemporary, they are; appropriate, they ain't. Not for this season anyway. The terms "classical" and "contemporary" cover a world of territory. More appropriate choices in a situation such as this one would be something by Strindberg for your classical piece, and something by David Rabe for your contemporary piece. It suits the aesthetic feel of our hypothetical theater's season's playwrights in far better fashion. Casting personnel have very specific needs they must meet. In appearance and audition material, help them to see you filling these needs. Or as my friend Ron Stetson of the Neighborhood Playhouse succinctly puts it, "You don't bring your baseball bat when you try out for the football team."

Besides looking at the appropriateness of your material and your apparel, let's go a little deeper. Does the material show you off to your best advantage? Does it let the casting director get to know who *you* are? Have you thought out and *really* prepared your material, so that you are giving a *performance,* and not just "doing a monologue"? Most actors do not spend anywhere near enough time working on their audition materials.

When I ask an actor who he's talking to in his monologue, most respond, "He's talking to his brother." And I say, "But who are *you* talking to? And what just happened? You were not born with the first line of the monologue!" Most actors cannot answer many questions they should be able to answer upon completion of a monologue. The most common flaws in auditioning stem not from lack of talent, but rather from a lack of *thought* and *preparation*.

We often hear the old saw that "casting directors have no imagination." This is a victim's attitude, and it's really not true. What casting directors don't have is the *time* to imagine what you might be able to do, if you looked the part and auditioned well with material that was suitable for the roles being cast. Casting directors are often casting several productions back-to-back. They have deadlines. And one other thing that everyone overlooks—they are running *businesses*. They have day-to-day headaches and pressures of running busy offices, besides the task at hand of casting. Please, don't expect them to take on the added burden of imagining what you might be capable of doing under the right circumstances. *Someone* will walk through the door who will give them what they need. Do the very best you can to make it be *you*!

There are teachers who specialize in the development of audition skills. These teachers advertise in trade papers. If you are not getting callbacks, interview with these teachers and find the right one for your needs. We can talk about the business of acting, but if you audition poorly, the "business" is a moot issue. You must get call-backs! If you are auditioning frequently and well, you will be. *To repeat: the best way of getting into an agent's office is to be invited in as a result of the agent's having seen your work.* But when you report high-level call-backs, your chances of finding an agent to consider representing you increase by a) calling you in as a result of the credibility you've been building, b) accepting an invitation to see you when you do perform (in Chapter 7, I will outline strategies for creating quality audition opportunities), or c) asking you to audition in the office, if they are unable to attend the production to which you invite them.

6

The Agent Interview

When you are scheduled for an appointment to meet with an agent, do not give the appearance that this is your one and only event of the day, even if it is! So often, I recall seeing young actors arrive twenty minutes early and overdressed for the occasion. There's no need to keep glancing nervously in the mirror to make sure everything is perfect for the big meeting, or to dress as if you are going to your sister's wedding after the interview is over. Relax. The specifics of what you wear are not necessarily as important as the effect you want to create. The effect you want to create is that, if we didn't know better, your appearance would lead everyone to believe that you are already working regularly and not necessarily seeking the services of an agent. Nice and clean casual is fine. Sloppy casual is not fine. Watch those shoes. Nothing blows an overall nice appearance faster than dusty, scuffy, or just plain down-at-the-heel shoes. Looks do count, especially in the acting business. If you doubt me on that score, look around and see which of your friends found representation the fastest.

At the risk of sounding superficial, I must stress just how visual the business of acting really is. I took part in many an agency meeting where one client's slight weight gain, or the progress of another client's bald spot became the topic of discussion. Look as good as you can. Cultivate some style. Watch what the actors who are your type and in the same age range as yourself are wearing in television commercials and in magazine advertising. I've heard color experts say that only one in four people look good in black, and yet three out of four of the actors I meet are swathed in it.

If you are a young man just out of college, don't wear a jacket and a tie to an interview with an agent. It's overdress, and it makes you look older. The same is true for young women. I have seen young women in their early twenties come to an agent's office in a dress, heels, and pearls. If you are in your early twenties and are just starting a professional acting career, the last thing you will want to do is to look like you are in your late twenties or early thirties. Arrive for the interview no more than ten minutes early, and try not to give the appearance that everything depends on this meeting. It doesn't, and the feeling that it does can be readily sensed.

While it is impossible to predict which direction the conversation will take, there are a few possibilities that I feel require preparation. The more prepared you are, the more relaxed you will be. And the more prepared you are, the more business-like you will come off, while you are giving the appearance of being casual and relaxed. The more effectively you answer the most commonly asked questions in the agent/actor interview, the better your chances of getting representation. The more you look like you feel you *belong* there—confident, not arrogant—

the better the response to you will be. I stress preparation here, because these meetings, depending on the agent's schedule or unforeseen interruptions, can be extremely brief. Unfortunately, a great many actors leave the agent/actor interview with extremely valuable information left unsaid. So let's prepare to "work" a good interview.

"TELL ME SOMETHING ABOUT YOURSELF"

Often, an agent will look at an actor and say, "Tell me something about yourself." This is the question most likely to make an actor squirm. Is that why it's asked so often? When I first started counseling actors in good business skills, I hesitated to devote time to a discussion of how to answer this query, thinking that actors would find it too minor to warrant attention. But they told me differently. As my services were sought more and more by actors at all professional levels, a discussion of this point became an almost daily occurrence. I decided it warranted attention when I saw a sea of heads nodding and eyes rolling when I brought it up at seminars. But the last straw was when an actor came to my office and told me he had recently been screen-tested for a popular prime-time television series. "I gave one of the best auditions I've ever given in my life," he said. "Right up until the very end, that is. And they said, "Now just look into the camera and TELL US SOMETHING ABOUT YOURSELF." The camera did not miss his thinly veiled exasperation when he said with a sigh, "Do you mean personal or professional?" Answering with another question is not an acceptable response here, although "Tell me something about yourself" is actually not a *question* at all. It is a *demand,* requiring a response, but the problem lies in its generality. It throws the ball right in your lap, and it's your move. "Tell me something about yourself" does not come up only in the entertainment industry, either. Ask anyone you know who has been job-hunting lately in *any* profession. It's everywhere. However, it happens to be especially irritating to an actor who has sometimes chosen the acting profession to avoid a discussion of this very issue.

Often, an actor will ask me, "What is it *they* want to know?" It's impossible to say what "they" want to know, since you only get asked this question by one person at a time. Since this individual isn't telling you specifically what she wants to know, we have to assume that she wants to get to know you a little better, and to see how you present yourself. The key to the answer to this "question" lies in its *preparation,* for if you do not have an answer prepared, you will not answer it well. So let's attend to it, and prepare for it, so that it will no longer be the dreaded invasion that it appears to be.

Most of the agents I know tell me that they like to get to know an actor, if only a little bit, before they discuss other areas. I especially find this true of casting directors who want to know what *you* are about, and how you might fit into the pieces of the casting puzzle. In other words, do not feel that you need to go right to the "sell" when you tell them "something about yourself." Saying, "Well, I just finished studying two years of Meisner Technique with Joe Smith, and before that I was at Strasberg for a year, and I've just found a great new voice teacher named Betty Anderson," does not particularly distinguish you from countless other actors around town—to say nothing of the fact that it's all probably on your resume anyway. Rather, go to the beginning, and briefly tell them where you are from, where you went to college if you did, when or how you got here—whichever may be more interesting— and then quickly bring them up-to-date on what's happening

professionally. Let them get to know *you* in your brief presentation. I'll give you an example.

Recently, an actor came to see me, and when I asked her to
"Tell me something about herself," she looked me right in the
eye, and with great charm and humor, she said: "I'm originally
from Providence, Rhode Island, where I grew up and attended
both grammar school and high school. I started dancing and
acting in school plays, but since my parents made it clear that
they did not think the performing arts was a feasible way to
make a living, I went to college—Boston University—and
studied biology. I never stopped dancing, though. Last spring, I
started sneaking down to New York on weekends to audition
for shows, and right after graduation I got lucky and landed my
first job in a summer tour of *42nd Street*. I just got back to the
city a few weeks ago, and I've started auditing classes with a
number of acting teachers. I'm happy to report that my parents
are adjusting beautifully!" Perfect! She needed no help from me
on this one. In one short minute, I learned where she was from,
a little about her background, that she had majored in science
at a New England university, and where she stood professionally at that moment. All bases covered!

I have met so many actors with fascinating backgrounds,
who grew up or went to school in places I've visited, have
worked with friends or professional colleagues, and all of it is
interesting to me, and potentially ice-breaking in the interview
situation. I have heard a few—very few—agents say they would
like a professional update at the start, but most prefer something along the lines of the presentation above. Also, it follows
an easier and more logical sequence to go in the order of beginning, middle, and end to your brief bio, rather than trying to
work backward from what happened most recently. More
important, if you make your presentation *concise* and *interest-*

ing, what difference does it make which information comes at the beginning, and which comes at the end if the whole thing only lasts a minute anyway? *Preparation* is the key. How you say it can be just as important as what you say, and your "sales pitch" began the moment you walked through the door. Preparation will allow you to tell them what you want them to know about you *in the way you want them to know it.* Take the time to prepare this, so that you will be brief, interesting, and business-like. I have heard from a number of actors who regretted that they did not attend to the preparation for this repeated inquiry.

"WHICH CASTING DIRECTORS KNOW YOUR WORK?"

This question is now coming up as often as not in the agent/actor interview, especially for the slightly seasoned actor. Answered well, it can be the most subtly powerful way to convince an agent to work with you. Unfortunately, it is almost *never* handled well by the actor. Let's analyze the question fully. In reality, what the agent is asking you is this: "How hard or easy a sell will you be? When I suggest your name to a casting director, who is going to say, 'Oh, she's great, send her over!' And who is going to say, 'Tell me about her!' "? (Translate: "Never heard of her, so if you want me to see her, start selling!")

But it goes deeper than that. In all the times I have asked this question, I have heard it answered well on only *one* occasion. The most frequent response I get is a short list, usually three names before the memory falters. I get no additional information regarding the specifics as to how the casting director knows the actor. When I probe further regarding the relationship between the actor and the casting director, I frequently discover that the actor has an impressive history (call-backs again!) with at least one, if not several, casting directors. However, I always find that the actor needs help in remembering which play, film, television series, or soap opera it was she got called back for, the role—this is almost always forgotten—and worse, the name of the casting director who auditioned her in the first place! Invariably, about an hour further into our session, when we've moved on to another topic, the actor will suddenly remember a long-forgotten close call with an important casting director. In real life, of course, it would be too late. If you have a good track record with any casting directors, you must be clear as a bell and sharp as a tack with this information when you are asked this question. Do not precede your response with a sheepish, "Oh, I'm *so* bad with names!" You cannot afford to be. Imagine a professional in any other field being asked who her contacts are, and responding in this fashion. Seems ludicrous, doesn't it? And yet, every day, I help actors recall the names of casting directors who called them back, screen-tested them, introduced them to the producers of the shows they almost got, which network it was, etc., etc. An agent does not have the time to do this with you, so it is up to you to be able to tell them.

Start with the names of those who have hired you. If no one has hired you yet, start with the names of those who have *almost* hired you, and what it was you almost got hired for. Be thorough. If you have auditioned for thirty projects, and gotten called back for only three of them, start with those three. Say something like this: "Jane Smith probably knows me best. She's auditioned and called me back to read for Treplev's understudy in the off-Broadway production of *The Seagull.* She also called me back when I auditioned for Peter in the New Haven Stage's production of *The Diary of Anne Frank,* as well as for Rolf in the Music Fair's production of *The Sound of Music.*" If there is another casting director who has also called you back, name him next, as in: "Jeff Jones also knows me. He read me twice for the recurring role of Tim Donovan on ABC's *The Young Doctors.*" Continue on down the list with another handful of names. Note that not one of the above situations resulted in a job, but they were all close calls. Very impressive. So rather than listing a couple of names of casting directors ("Jane Smith, Jeff Jones," etc.), whom for all the agent knows you may have met at a paid seminar—you will be telling an agent that these casting directors not only *know* your work, they *like* your work, too. When you list your strengths first, you are also telling an agent that you have a history of close calls, that you audition well, and given more chances at bat—with the agent's help, of course!—you will probably land a job, and thereby pay her a commission($).

You should have a casual and off-the-cuff delivery with this presentation. Don't sound memorized and robot-like. It can be a very powerful sales tool. Just make it a "soft-sell." The more recent the good response, the stronger the impression, of course. Still any close calls within the past couple of years can head the list. Sometimes an actor doesn't meet up with certain casting directors more often than that. Don't concern yourself here with whether or not the casting director whose name you are mentioning will remember you. This is a very common and understandable fear on the actor's part. You are not guaranteeing the agent that the casting director will remember you, but by telling the absolute truth, well-presented, you are saying, in effect: "When I met this casting director, the response was good. If you send me there again, this time she may like me even more, I may get the job, and make some money for you." Also, reporting call-backs is the most likely information to be used by an agent when she is trying to "pitch" you to a casting director who does not yet know you—as I illustrated in the last chapter. Remember Sandra and her call-backs for *Les Miserables*?

Earlier, I mentioned that I had met only one actor who had answered the question of which casting directors knew his work as well as it could have been answered. The actor, whose name was Jim, told me that he had been auditioning especially well at the EPAs of late, and had been called back on three projects in recent weeks. When an agent he met asked him who "knew his work," he responded with a complete, yet concise history of his recent track record—which included the names of the casting directors, the roles he read for, and the number of call-backs. So sharp and clear was he, that the agent responded: "You just said all the right names. Let's find some projects to submit you on right away." Again, not all agents will leap into action in this way without having seen your work, but more would than you might think. In his delivery, what the actor was saying to the agent was: "Your buyers—those whom you must get on the phone and sell to day in and day out—already *know* me and *like* me." The agent's response was, in effect: "If my buyers like you—and you made it clear that they do—there is nothing further I need to know about you. I will start working with you today!"

In order to make record keeping of this kind easy, I have devised a simple method to keep all of this information on a single page or two. List it in descending order of for whom and for what you have gotten the best response. (See Appendix C.) Note that the first category says, "Casting Director." It may be, however, that you were hired, called back, or auditioned by the director or artistic director of a particular theater. If that is the case, list it in the first category anyway, with a notation next to this person's name, along with her position. I have heard actors say "None" when they are asked which casting directors know their work. An investigation reveals that they have been hired—or almost hired—by well-known directors. If this is the case, be sure to say so. Even if you've done very little, and do not know any casting directors yet, say: "Mainly, I've been cast by the directors of the plays that I've been in—such as Joe Smith who cast me in *Hurlyburly,* and Tom Andrews who directed me in *Isn't It Romantic?*" Obviously, the better known the director, the stronger the impression. Nevertheless, do the best you can, and name a couple of names you think the agent might be familiar with. Even if she is not familiar with them, you will have responded in a more intelligent and business-like manner than if you had said, "None."

In order to implement the Casting Director listing for best results, keep a few spaces between each name on the list so you can slot in the latest response in its appropriate place. That is, keep the names of those who have *hired* you in first position, those who have almost hired you in second position, and those for whom you have auditioned more than once but not been called back by in the next position. In last place, keep the names of those for whom you have only auditioned once. Although slots are provided for the dates, you will see that the list is not kept chronologically. It is kept in order of "credibility." You will need to revamp it periodically of course, but you will have your casting directors in a consolidated fashion, at your fingertips, and stacked in order, ready for verbal presentation. While I stress that this system is to prepare you for a verbal presentation, an actor recently reported to me that she had taken the list out and started reading it to an agent who asked her who her casting contacts were! Nevertheless, the agent was delighted with her strong response and organizational skills, and proceeded to make a photocopy of her list to keep on file with her photos and resumes. So, if you are not as comfortable in the interview as you might have hoped, it is better to take out the list than to leave valuable information unsaid.

"WHAT HAVE YOU BEEN DOING LATELY?"

The question of who knows your work may take another form. You may be asked, "What's been happening for you professionally lately?" Or words to that effect. This question will still give you the opportunity to bring up the names of those who know and like you. If you have attended twenty auditions in the last ten weeks, and been called back for only four, talk about those in addition to any work you have been doing. Go to your strengths. Leaving the negative things outside the door is very hard, but that is what you must do. It's the nature of the business of acting that most of the time you don't get the part. This happens at every level. But I am amazed at how much digging I have to do when I am working with an actor to get to the "good stuff" that has been happening. Agents and casting directors do not have the time to do this, nor is it their job. I think many actors fear that if they state their best case for themselves, an agent will look at them and say, "BIG DEAL! I HAVE CLIENTS WHO HAVE DONE MUCH MORE THAN THAT!! TWO OF MY ACTORS GOT NOMINATED FOR TONY AWARDS THIS YEAR!!" And, sad to say, there are a few agents out there who just might respond like that. But most will not.

Make the most of yourself. That's what a good agent does for her clients. Do it for yourself, and most agents will respond in kind. If you fear that talking about how close you've gotten on some auditions sounds boastful, remember this: Agents are in a bottom-line business. Sales. A strong track record of close calls and good relationships with casting directors and directors will be music to the ears of most people in the agency business. After all, something got you in the door, and now you will want to show them that their instincts about you are shared by those who actually do the hiring. And if "stacking the deck" in your favor—when you list your contacts—has a manipulative ring, remember that it will help the agent to know how casting personnel "see" you in terms of which kinds of roles you are most likely to play. This is all-important and may lead to one of the most commonly asked questions of all.

"HOW DO YOU SEE YOURSELF?"

When an agent asks this question, she usually has some idea as to what kinds of roles she might submit you for. But is your concept of how you are likely to be cast in sync with hers? If not, your chances of being represented by this agent may start to diminish. I am astounded at the number of actors who respond to this question with: "I see myself playing roles like Nicole Kidman or Julia Roberts gets." Or "I see myself playing roles like Brad Pitt or Tom Cruise gets." There are a couple of built-in problems with this more-common-than-you-might-believe response. Personally, I have no problem with the unrealistic, stratospheric career levels being cited here, as I think anyone entering the business of acting should be ambitious as hell. But one should exercise caution in identifying oneself with those who conjure up the image of the ultimate in romantic and sexual appeal. That is, of course, unless this state of affairs is pretty much verified and reinforced in your everyday dealings with the world at large. Actually, the more one genuinely has this kind of appeal, the less one will be asked how one "sees" oneself. How you will be perceived and how you will be cast will be all too apparent. And the more one truly projects this kind of appeal, the briefer one's search for representation will be.

This is not to say that one cannot cite a "prototype" when answering the "how do you see yourself?" question. This business loves prototypes. When a casting director puts out a role description on Breakdown Services, it very often carries with it a tag line, such as: "We are looking for a Kevin Costner or Harrison Ford type." Or "We are looking for a Goldie Hawn or Meg Ryan type."

The problem with citing a prototype often lies with a lack of specificity. Let's say, for example, that you are an actor who has been likened—in appearance and manner—to Glenn Close. You hear it all the time. To respond: "I see myself as a Glenn Close type" is insufficient—Glenn Close has performed a great range of roles. You may be the same "type" as Ms. Close, but what kind of roles do you play well? And if you would be cast similarly to Glenn Close, in which of those roles would you be best cast? Would it be the dominating, calculating Merteuil in *Dangerous Liaisons,* or would it be the moralistic, contentious Annie in Tom Stoppard's play *The Real Thing*? Or maybe you'd be at your best in a role like that crackpot she played in *Fatal Attraction.* This is a wide range.

If you do not have a "prototype," examine what your own best work has been. Do this even if you are still only an acting student. What kinds of roles does your teacher assign you for scene work? What are the characteristics of the roles you've felt best suited for or have gotten the best response to in performance? What adjectives would you use to describe them? Are they blue-collar workers? Or blue-blood aristocrats? Eccentric and quirky? Or earthy and grounded? If you feel that you can play a substantial range of roles especially well, name a couple of the roles and the plays that illustrate your point.

Even those who have the awareness to see themselves as character actors will often say: "I know I'm not a romantic leading lady (or man), but I'm good at roles like the funny friend or the funny neighbor." Whose funny friend? What funny neighbor? They're not all the same. In other words, name the traits, or characteristics, that describe the roles you feel you will be best cast in—that is, in addition to any proto-type you might fit. Think the question of "how you see your-self" through. Ask for *brutally* honest input from teachers and friends. You may as well get it from them, because you will certainly get it from some agents. Prepare a response, but by all means be *concise*. A good specific response to this ques-tion reflects intelligence, self-awareness, and a business-like approach to the product and service you are marketing. I am convinced that the most successful and *happiest* actors know themselves, know what they do best, and know where they fit in—all with remarkable clarity.

The idea is to give them a *handle* on you—on where you best fit in, and, therefore, how to "move" you. In order to express range without being all over the place—agents tend to *dislike* it when actors say, "Oh, my range is so wide, I can play so many different kinds of roles, blah, blah, blah"—your response should have a running theme, and you should try to *lean* in a specific direction. In doing so, you're not really oblit-erating anything else you can do; you're simply giving them a good grasp on you.

Ideally then, think about roles that are a combination of what you do *best* and roles that *also* blend with your own essence. So you might say, "I tend to be cast as characters who are independent, strong willed, and down-to-earth. For example, one of my best roles was Martha Livingstone, the psychiatrist in *Agnes of God*. In a lighter vein, I've also played Heidi in *The Heidi Chronicles*. She's another self-reliant, strong, and intelligent character. Also, people have often compared me with Susan Sarandon, and I can see myself being cast in the *kinds of roles* she's often played—especially *as a character like* Louise in *Thelma and Louise.*"

If you have a prototype who is a film star, as in the above case, fine. If you don't, I think it's unwise to force one. However, if you do have one, *link* your prototype to a specific role for purposes of clarity. Also, notice in the last example, where a film star is cited, that I have emphasized the words *kinds of roles* and *as a character like.* I'm suggesting that you do, too. Here's why: While most agents would encourage the kind of example I've illustrated, without this emphasis, some could misconstrue your answer to mean that you see yourself at a career level to be considered for such major film roles. When you're discussing plays, it's not a problem, as many actors will play the roles you cite. But for films, it's wise to clarify your point.

Okay, now let's go back and look at your answer. You'll see repetition of characteristics (stated slightly differently, of course), but you'll also see that the roles themselves are actually quite varied. You've stated versatility and range without being scattered and unfocused. So there is a running theme. The idea is to go for the *characteristics* and the *essence* of the roles, using similar adjectives, and then *slide* over using "leaning" terminology such as "on the lighter side" or "only with a more humorous bent," etc. Speak in *gradations* when you're sliding to different roles by using terminology such as "darker" or "even slightly quirkier," etc. This approach will ease you into talking about a role that is *different* from the previous role you've mentioned, but it still allows you to point out how they are similar.

Let's try one for a hypothetical male actor, who might say something like this: "The general profile of roles in which I'm cast seems to fit in a category of what I would call 'outsiders'— ranging from very dark, edgy, even dangerous characters like Pale in *Burn This!*, which is a role that I've done, to the far less dark and more poetic 'outsider' of Tom in *The Glass Menagerie*. In fact, directors and casting directors have remarked that I'm similar in sensibility to John Malkovich, who, of course, has played both these roles. On the more humorous side, but still dark and edgy and very quirky, would be a role *similar to the character* Christopher Walken played in the film *Biloxi Blues*."

Okay, are there similar characteristics here? Yes. Is there range? Yes. Is it confusing and all over the place? No. Note that I've mentioned *two* prototypes in the above presentation. Try to limit this approach to instances where there is a similarity in sensibility between the two prototypes—as would be the case with Malkovich and Walken.

Often when I'm working on this issue with an actor, I'll start by saying, "If I had ten million dollars, and I was willing to produce a production on Broadway of any play you've ever done, and everyone in the entertainment industry would see your work, which play would you pick? And what role did you play? Why would you choose this play and this role? What is this character like?"

After we examine the first play the actor chooses, I might say, "Fine, let's try another. This time let's look at a comedy [or a drama]." It's fun to watch a pattern emerge.

As you think about these questions, remember that the roles you cite in preparation for the "How do you see yourself?"

question don't necessarily have to be roles that you have *already* played; it's just a sensible option that you might use depending on the body of work that you've done.

Unfortunately, very few actors have an intelligent response prepared for this question. Yet actors who regularly work almost always do. Why? Well, because they have solid careers and are employed most of the time, it's not hard for them to cite the ways in which they tend to be cast. The point here is that *you're* trying to get into *their* league, and presenting yourself as well as they do creates a powerful perception of you.

For the most part, the usual response to this question that agents get from an aspiring or unestablished actor is a stunned look followed by a blank stare off to the left, while the actor's expression reads, "Hmm, I've never really thought about that. I wonder what that means. Let me see. . . ." Then the actor takes a long pause and fumbles for something intelligent to say. Let me stress that from an agent's point of view, this is not impressive.

Having once been an actor, I can understand and appreciate that you don't sit around all day thinking about "how you see yourself"; you are busy working on your work (although a part of this is, of course, to know yourself!). Agents, however, regularly pose this question as a marketing screen, and you need to have a thoughtful, intelligent response—one that is both clear *and* concise. In a recent discussion ten agents said that actors' lack of clarity about who they are and where they realistically fit in is singularly the biggest problem that they encounter in working with actors.

I know of a few agents who phrase this question slightly differently: "Name a role in a current production on or off-Broadway where you could replace the actor who is playing the role if he (or she) were to leave the show." Wow! You can consider this version of the query to be a combination of *two* questions: (1) "How do you see yourself?" and (2) "How abreast are you of what's going on in the business?" So do your homework. I find that "How do you see yourself?" is the question *most* dreaded by actors. Don't be afraid of it; *prepare* for it.

Note well: Everyone isn't going to see you the same way, so please don't risk paralyzing your activity by *over*analyzing this agent-oriented issue. Live theater allows you the greatest flexibility of range (age, physicality etc.). Therefore, *show up* for every audition that you think you're right for, give the best audition you can, and know that the "business" will guide you to where you belong, because in the final analysis, that's how it really works. *Trust it.*

THE OFFICE AUDITION

Whether or not you have been told in advance to prepare audition material for a meeting with an agent, you must be prepared to perform at any time. If you are new to the business of acting and have few credits on your resume, or perhaps have just finished acting school, it is likely that the agent will already know that about you. There is nothing wrong with being in either of these categories, but there is something very wrong with not being prepared to show your acting skills to any industry professional who may ask to see them.

Recently, an actor whose theatrical credentials were quite impressive told me that in the course of an interview with one of New York's top agents, he asked if she might be willing to try to get him an audition for an upcoming production that was about to be cast. She replied that she would be willing to try to get him seen, but since she did not have firsthand knowledge of his abilities—this meeting had been arranged by referral—would he perform a monologue for her? A completely understandable request. He told her that he was working on some new pieces that were not quite ready, so could he come back the next week and perform at that time? She said that he could, and to telephone her later in the week to set up an appointment. (Note: this actor was now seeking a *second* appointment, thus more of this lady's time.) When he telephoned her at week's end, she was unable to re-schedule him right away, and suggested that he call her again the following week. He called her a few more times, was unable to reach her, the communication weakened, and he was never re-scheduled. "A terrible thing to do to an actor, isn't it?" he asked me. "Promise to see someone, and not keep your word!" "Robert," I said, "you blew it!" And Robert agreed that I was right. Assume that you *can't* come back another time. If someone you want to meet grants you an interview, that *is* your time. Remember, it's also *their* time.

Many good actors become somewhat unglued when asked to perform in someone's office. Thrown off guard, they start a litany of questions, usually beginning with, "Should I just do it sitting right here?" To which an agent will probably respond, "Whatever is comfortable for you." Translate: "If you don't give a damn how you perform, I sure don't." Get up! Claim some space! I have never seen a monologue that worked better when the actor was beached in a chair—especially the same chair she's been interviewed in for the preceding fifteen minutes—than when she got up and created some space for herself. Not that it's highly advantageous to get out of the chair you're sitting in and walk three feet away, pull up another chair, and sit in that one to do your monologue, either!

Remember in the last chapter we talked about the importance of *giving a performance,* rather than "doing a monologue"? This is no less true when you audition for an agent. When you audition for an agent, you are saying, in effect: "Based on what you see me do in the next couple of minutes, invest in me. Send out my photos and resumes repeatedly. Send them by costly messenger service if necessary. Get on the telephone and convince casting directors to meet with me. Do this often and passionately, and someday I will be able to pay you ten cents on my every earned dollar. When I get a job. *If* I get a job." Bearing this in mind, you will not wish merely to "do a monologue."

Another question: "Should I use you, or look someplace else?" Most agents prefer *not* to be looked at, as it forces them to become your "scene partner," which makes them uncomfortable. It will probably make you uncomfortable too, as you will most likely be unable to avoid monitoring their response to what you are doing. For example, if you are doing a comedic monologue and find a stone-face looking back at you, will this serve you in any way? I think not. A good choice is to imagine that the character to whom you are speaking is standing directly behind where the agent is seated—facing you. The agent will be seated, and you will be standing. She can then watch you, as you talk to your "scene partner." Since your scene partner is standing *behind* her, it will be pretty easy for the agent to lose sight of the fact that there is no one there! This will enable you to use all the space in your area of the office, without fear of upstaging yourself in any way whatsoever. The eyes of your imaginary scene partner will be straight across from yours and a couple of feet above the agent's head. You will then be looking right in the *direction* of the agent, yet not directly *at* her. Of course, you will not be staring directly into the eyes of your scene partner, but you will always know exactly where they are, when you wish to "check his reaction" to what you are saying. I've experimented with this dozens of times. When you perform a monologue this way, your auditor can see your face and your eyes perfectly. Some actors, bending over backwards *not* to "use" the agent, make choices that do them a great disservice, and end up hiding half their faces while they talk to no one in the corner of the room. There are some people who do like to be used. But most don't. Besides, if you perform your monologue in the way I have suggested, they can see all that they need to, perfectly well, which is all that should concern them. After all, it's *your* performance, so it should be *your* choice. You are the one who must rise to the challenge of being focused *and* relaxed at the same time!

But who is this scene partner? The best choice is someone *you* really know. Someone with whom you can make the monologue connect emotionally. A good monologue is really a *scene,* and a relationship full of meaning is your goal here. It is the easiest thing in the world to detect a lack of specificity of relationship in the monologue audition. And when you have completed your monologue, don't "break character" as you are saying your last word! This is so destructive to what you have created. See your scene partner's reaction to your last line—in other words, let that last line "land." Think of *The Tonight Show.* Notice when a guest brings a short clip of a new film she's plugging, it's usually a well-chosen scene. Think of how the scene ends. One character (usually the guest on the show!) throws her last line at the other character. The line "lands," the frame freezes, and your television screen goes gray for a second—then we quickly cut back to the host, who does a take, and the house comes down! That impact is what you want to create when you finish your monologue.

SELECTING MATERIAL

What kind of material should one choose for the office audition? It certainly should be something you do especially well, and it should also be something that suits the needs of the agent for whom you are auditioning. If this agent represents actors for film and television, don't do anything from the classics. Even for agents who handle theater, good contemporary material is usually their preference. That is not to say that the theater actor should not have classical material prepared, of course, but it probably won't make a good first choice. If you are asked to perform classical material, brevity is appreciated. Especially if it's Shakespeare. Avoid explosive, highly charged emotional material in the office audition. Remember, there are probably other office personnel—as well as those on the other end of the telephone conversations in which they may be engaged—who could find themselves the uncomfortable parties to your ear-splitting angst. You may be asked to do two contemporary monologues—one comedic, and one dramatic. If you are asked for one monologue, and you feel equally skilled with comedic and dramatic material, I recommend doing the comedic piece. As a general rule of thumb, unless it is inappropriate to the situation, I think comedic material is a better choice. It's entertaining, seductive, and, out of the context of an entire play, flies well. An audition is a *result*-oriented situation. People have long flocked to clubs or watched television shows where performers come out for a few minutes to make them laugh. Clubs and TV shows where performers come out and do dramatic monologues are not yet the rage. This tells us something about the inherent appeal of comedy. Especially in the middle of an agent's workday.

Important, too, is to pick material from a role in which you would be likely to be cast. The agent audition/interview is a marketing situation, and "how you see yourself" will be reflected in your choice of audition material.

THE RELATIONSHIP BEGINS

When an actor in New York has been seen in performance by an agent—onstage or in the office—the agent will sometimes want to try the actor out on a few auditions before offering to "sign" the actor. This is known as freelancing, and many New York agents and actors keep this loose arrangement indefinitely. Many New York actors are freelancing with several agents, who only need to "clear" the actor when they have a project for which they feel the actor may be suited. This is *not* the policy in Los Angeles, however, where actors and agents work together on an exclusive signed-only basis. Or as Los Angeles agents put it, "We marry out here, we don't date."

In the event that an agent—New York or Los Angeles—expresses an immediate desire to sign you to a contract, make sure you have explored your options before signing. At the very least, you will want to take the contracts home, look them over, and discuss with the agent anything that is not clear to you. If you have more than one agency that has set up an appointment to meet with you, tell the first agent that you are happy about her offer and will give it strong consideration, but that you are unable to make a decision just yet, as you have other appointments with agents that are still outstanding. You will then undoubtedly be asked with whom else you will be meeting. I see no advantage in not telling the agent who the others are, and you can be sure that this will make you even more desirable. However, the agent may proceed to tell you how much more she will be able to do for you than the agents whose names you have mentioned. A really sharp New York agent who wants to sign you will start to "clear" you on projects immediately when informed that you are meeting with others, as she may now be competing with them. For example, if you have a meeting with Agent A on Monday who wants to sign you, and you must postpone making a decision because you have meetings with Agents B and C on Thursday and Friday, you may hear from Agent A a number of times before Thursday and Friday roll around. This may be Agent A's way of swaying you into thinking that she is the agent that will do the most for you *before* you have even had a chance to meet with Agents B and C. This is not necessarily just a ploy on Agent A's part; it may come from a genuinely enthusiastic response to you. However, it is also not necessarily an indication of the shape of things to come, as agents have been known to indiscriminately submit actors on projects for which they are not ideally suited as a way of leading them to believe that if the actor will commit, there will be a boundless supply of opportunities in store.

If you find yourself in the very fortunate position of having more than one agent who is pressing you to sign, you will need to weigh a few factors before making your decision. The most important factor is to try to determine which agent you feel will do her best to provide you with the greatest number of opportunities to be seen for the roles for which you are best suited. In order to make an intelligent assessment in this regard, it will be of utmost importance that you and your prospective agent discuss the kinds of roles that *both* you and she feel are the roles in which you are most likely to be cast. Presuming you are in agreement here, you will also want to assess how much enthusiasm the agent has demonstrated in expressing her desire to represent you. Let me give you an example. Recently, a very smart young actor I know completed a three-year contract role on a top-rated daytime soap opera in Los Angeles. He had the opportunity to meet with several agents at the largest and most "powerful" talent agencies in the entertainment industry, all of whom offered to sign him exclusively. He decided to stay with the smaller agent who had launched his career. "While I felt that the larger agencies may have had more access to the powers that be, I didn't feel any real *enthusiasm* on their part," he said. "In other words, I wasn't confident that a lot of energy was going to go toward my career, and if things didn't work out, no one would really care. The opposite has always been true with my present agent, however. He fights tooth and nail to get me seen for everything he possibly can, does a great job of it, and is boundlessly enthusiastic and aggressive. So I stayed." I must point out here that this actor's decision was based strictly on what he felt was in his best interest—as an actor in business for himself. Loyalty was *not* a consideration. His contractual time with his agent had expired; he had paid the full commissions this agent was due, and was free to make any career choice he wished with regard to representation. Had he felt that one of the larger agencies would have served his career needs better at this time, he would have made his decision accordingly. However, it was his *instinct,* as well as his past experience with his agent, of course, that led him to his decision.

Ideally, then, an actor is looking for an agent who will try to get him as many auditions as possible—for the roles for which he is best suited, as well as at a career level that he can realistically expect. To assess the career levels at which a prospective agent represents clients, visit IMDbPro.com (there is a free trial available at this *industry* version of the Internet Movie Database) and search for the agency. This link will pull up the agency's client list, and each client's name is a link to that actor's profile and career history. It will be helpful to know not only which actors are handled by an agency where you have a meeting scheduled, but in which media these actors regularly work. After weighing these factors, you will be in a better position to make a decision as to which agency you want to represent you. Agency contracts have been drawn up by the unions, which means that they lean more in the actor's favor than in the agency's. In fact, agency contracts are terminable on the part of either the agent *or* the actor if the actor has not worked or received specified compensation for work within the number of days as set by the unions. For current information regarding the number of days and the amount of compensation involved—New York and Los Angeles contracts differ—contact the Screen Actors Guild.

More common than either party terminating a current contract, however, is a sad lack of communication on the part of the actor with his representative. All too often, an actor will see his friends going to auditions for which he feels he should also be scheduled. He will say nothing about it for the longest time, and when the situation becomes no longer bearable, he will fire an angry call or email to his agent. Or worse, the actor will schedule a long-overdue meeting with his agent, and explode over these slights and injustices—thus ending a potentially salvageable relationship. By virtue of the fact that an actor is a signed agency client, it is not just his right, but it is also his responsibility to communicate his feelings to his agent. If your agent is unwilling to communicate with you, it is indeed time to consider the need for other representation.

Earlier, I mentioned that in New York, it is a more common occurrence that an agent who has been impressed with your work will freelance with you to see what the response to you is like from at least a few casting directors. Monitoring response is commonly known as "getting feedback"—a term that I never liked, as it sounds like some screeching sound that is emitted when two pieces of audio-electronic equipment are placed too close to one another. A part of me feared that if I called a casting director and asked for "feedback" she might push some button on her telephone that would make a hellish noise that would send me flying out of my chair. Therefore, getting "response" was my term of choice. Now there can be a number of reasons why an agent may not be prepared to enter into a signed agreement with you—not the least of which may be an economic slowdown during which she has been unable to get a lot of activity for those clients to whom she is already committed, and who may have in the past (or present) paid her sizable commissions. She may also feel that you are a specific "type" of performer, one for whom she does not anticipate getting a large number of auditions. In a case such as this, the agent may see no benefit—on your part or hers—of a signed agreement.

The most unfortunate result of an interview with an agent who has expressed a sincere interest in working with you on a freelance basis—after seeing your work—is that no such relationship develops. It is also an everyday occurrence. It often happens that an actor is called in to meet with an agent who has seen him perform (the best way in, in my view!). The agent spends a half hour talking with the actor, enthusiastically introduces him to associates, and then asks the actor to leave a dozen photos. Upon departure, the actor is assured that he will be called and "cleared" for the next role for which the agent feels he is suited. And the actor never hears from the agent again! What happened? Let's analyze this common and unfortunate situation, and learn how to take measures to avoid it.

Why would an agent call an actor into her office after seeing him perform, spend a long time with him, wax enthusiastic about his performance, introduce him around the office, and ask for a pile of photos and resumes if she had no intention of working with him? She wouldn't. When an actor relates this puzzling and disappointing experience to me, I ask: "How did *you* close the meeting? What did you say regarding the exact manner in which you would be working together? How did you follow up? What did you do?" Actually, no one has to tell me. Usually, a promising meeting of this kind ends with the actor saying his thank-yous, expressing his delight, and bolting out of the office before saying something that he feels might destroy the good impression that he's made. This is followed up on the actor's part by a thank-you note, again expressing delight "to be working together," and then telephoning the agent to "check in"—to which the agent usually responds, "Nothing now." The actor then sends a few photo postcards to the agent, still doesn't hear anything, soon decides that the agent was insincere, and starts looking for representation anew.

Now let's look at this situation from the *agent's* perspective. When an agent expresses a desire to freelance with an actor whose work—on the stage, demo reel, or in the office audition—she has liked, she usually means it *when she is saying it.* What she is not thinking about is that in reality there may be a number of circumstances that could prevent her from thinking about you when a role for which you may be suited is being cast. Even the most organized talent agency is a hectic arena, with agents juggling several phone calls at once—trying to meet the demands of their present clients, as well as those of the casting directors. And any ambitious agent will probably be meeting other talented actors—some of whom she may like as much as she liked you. Further, it is not an agent's *responsibility* to think about an actor with whom she does not have a commitment. Therefore, when an agent has responded favorably to your work, and expresses what you perceive to be a sincere interest in freelancing with you, it will probably be necessary for you to propose the guidelines by which you will proceed to communicate with her.

Let me illustrate with an example of how a young actor handled this very situation in the best possible way. Some years ago, when I was representing actors, a signed client telephoned and asked me if I would see a friend of his whom he felt was very talented and in need of agent representation. This is a request which, as I mentioned in Chapter 5, is frequently granted as a courtesy gesture. I suggested to my client that he have his friend call me to arrange a meeting. A few days later, I interviewed this young actor, who was then a college student and is now a successful film actor. While I found him a charming and personable guy, I was unable to get a clear sense of the kind of roles for which he might be suited. My instinct told me that he was probably not untalented, but I essentially dismissed him by telling him I would have to see him in performance before I would be able to consider representing him in any way. (An important note here: had I felt very strongly about this actor's potential, if only in terms of "type," I would have asked him to perform in the office.) He countered by telling me that he was then in rehearsal for a school production. I told him that because the client who had referred him was in the play also, I would be attending. As it turned out, this actor had a rather small role, but his work was impressive. When I saw him backstage, I suggested that he bring photos to my office the following week, and I would see what I could do for him.

When he came by early on the following Monday morning, I again expressed my (at the moment) sincere interest in helping him, but told him that in all honesty, I was not sure how many auditions I would be able to get for him. Nevertheless, I would do my best to keep him in mind. Hardly a commitment on my part. He said: "*If* I should hear about something *specific* that is being cast, and there is a role in it for which I feel I am *really well suited,* may I call or email you to discuss my being submitted?" Since I had seen and liked his work, and felt that what he was asking was not especially demanding, I agreed to this arrangement. Note that this actor did *not* say what actors so often say to an agent: "What is the best way for me to keep in touch with you?" This is not assertive enough, and the agent just might say, "Keep in touch with postcards, and let me know what you are doing." Congratulations, you just gave all your power away. No, this actor expressed his wishes in a way that assured me that he was not going to be hounding me indiscriminately.

A few weeks later he emailed and reminded me of our agreement, and suggested an idea to me. He told me about a specific play that was soon to be cast. He said there was a character in the play who was twenty years old. He himself was then twenty-one. Then he told me the name of the director, of whom I had never heard. He said that this director had cast him in a one-performance reading of another play two years before. He said that the director had liked his work in this reading, and would probably remember him. Would I submit him for the role? Of course I would. Why not? This actor had done my work for me. He was *aware*—in advance of the play's being cast; he was *specific*—about both the play and the role; and he gave me a *reason* to submit him. Not only was he the right age for the role, but the director already knew and liked him.

Here was a young actor who knew what he wanted, and, perhaps more important, knew how to ask for what he wanted.

Simple and logical as this may seem, most actors are unable to do it well, because they lack the necessary information. While you should always be as aware of what is going on as you possibly can, and specific about what you are asking for, having a reason may at times present a challenge. In the next chapter, I'll talk about how to research the theatrical season well in advance; how to find out who will be casting what; and as best as possible, how to discover whether or not there is a role for which you might be suited. In addition, I will discuss ways to create audition opportunities—from showcase to Broadway. If you are auditioning well through open calls and Equity principal auditions, you will, at the very least, be getting called back. These call-backs alone can constitute a very strong reason for an agent to be willing to submit you for projects when they are being done by these and other casting directors. But you must bring this information to them. Then you will be approaching agents with your hand *full*, and not your hand *out*. When you operate in this way, you are making something in it for *them*, not just you. And this is the secret of being a good businessperson. A good salesperson.

The young actor in the above story seemed to come by this naturally. He always approached things this way. While an agent smarter than I actually signed him, his later success came as no surprise to me. When an agent likes your work, ask if you can work with him in this way. If his interest in you is sincere, he will most likely agree. Many actors who have consulted with me privately have reported enormously gratifying results when they have made this adjustment at the close of a good interview with an agent who represents actors for theater, film, and television. Some actors have several agencies with whom they are freelancing. This will probably continue until one of these relationships grows stronger than the others. In between phone calls with specific projects in mind, they keep their relation-ships strong by reporting their progress by mail. This makes an agent to whom they have not spoken in a while more likely to speak with them when they call. This is especially the case when they have reported *true* career progress.

7

What's Going On? Who's Casting What? Theater and Film

THEATER

Whether working in conjunction with an agent or not, it is of utmost importance to be *aware* of what is going on, and to know who will be doing what—as far in advance of the casting process as possible. One of the most common and unfortunate situations actors find themselves in is learning crucial casting information *too late*. Often, an actor will lament that had he been *aware* that a casting director who knows him, or a director with whom he had once worked, was casting a production, he would have been able to secure an audition. But plays generally do not produce, cast, direct, and find theaters in which to house themselves overnight. In the theater, most of this information is made available well in advance of production. The wise actor knows well ahead of time which productions will be mounted, who will be casting them, and, as best he can, whether there are roles for which he might be suited. Such actors are rare, but they do exist. Not coincidentally, it is this same actor who is often employed, as well. In the last chapter, we met one such actor; let me tell you about another.

Recently, an actor came to see me to discuss career matters that did not include unemployment. Despite lack of representation, she had been working on Broadway for nearly ten straight years without interruption—another rarity. In the course of our meeting, I asked her if she was *aware* of the *specifics* of the upcoming theatrical season. She not only knew which productions were planned for both on Broadway and off, but in some cases, such as revivals of former productions, she had already read the play. Where the proposed production was based on material from another source, such as a novel, she had read the novel. If the production being planned was based on a popular film, she had rented the film, and knew if there was a role for her. In addition, she knew the names of most of the casting directors who had been hired to cast these productions and the approximate start dates. It was easy to see why she had not seen the unemployment line in nearly a decade.

Even for the student, or beginning actor, who may not yet feel ready to compete at this level, I recommend developing this habit of long-range awareness in the earliest stages of one's career. I would not expect an actor to know from the start all that will be happening in the theater, well in advance. It is a habit one must work to develop so that it becomes second nature. Then it's easy. However, if it feels like too much homework and research to trouble yourself with, remember the actors in the above story and at the end of the last chapter. They are the stuff your *real* competition is made of!

.   .   .

How did the actor above know so much so far in advance? Let's take a look at some of the resources available, and perhaps more importantly, *learn how to use them.*

Theatrical Index

First, *Theatrical Index*. In publication for over forty years, this weekly is an invaluable source of information. Agents rely on it heavily: each Monday, twenty-three copies of it are sent to the William Morris Agency alone. Other regular subscribers include: Dustin Hoffman, Al Pacino, and Barbra Streisand, as well as casting directors, directors, and producers on both coasts. *Theatrical Index* is available at theater bookstores in New York City, as well as through full and partial subscriptions from its publisher (see Appendix E).

Each week, *Theatrical Index* chronicles both current and *future* productions, on Broadway and off, tracks the itinerary of national touring companies, and provides crucial data regarding current and *future* productions at numerous regional theaters throughout the United States. It also includes news of the Canadian and London theater scenes as well. In addition to listing the names and locations of scheduled productions, the *Index* also furnishes the names of playwrights, producers, directors, and in most cases, the names of the casting directors of these productions. In instances where the major roles have already been cast, the stars' names are listed, along with dates of the start of rehearsals, previews, and opening.

Theatrical Index is a weekly publication; updates are reported as they are received. For this reason, I *recommend getting it at least once a month—to develop as long-range an overview as possible.* This is ongoing research. If agents with all their alleged power and contacts need this information in order to request auditions on their clients' behalf, surely you will need it to communicate with agents and casting directors on your own behalf. The more advanced in your career you are, the more you will find names of casting directors, playwrights, and producers who know you. With or without representation, the more you know about what's being done, who will be doing it, and what will be needed, the more audition opportunities you will be able to create.

Note the names of the casting directors of current and future productions. You will see that certain names keep recurring. These are known—by me anyway—as the "biggies." Often there will be a brief description of the play, and the number of characters in it. If the production is a revival or has been performed before, as is the case with many Broadway productions, especially musicals, the *Index* will include specifics of its original production (opening date, theater it played at, etc.). This is of utmost importance, for in many cases, it will mean that the work has already been published. If so, get the play and see if there is a role for which you might be suited. For new plays or musicals, you will very often see, as mentioned earlier, that the project has been adapted from another source, such as a novel, short story, or film. Research into these sources themselves will provide you with more specific character information. *If a production appears to have already been cast, remember that the nature of the business dictates that cast names are often tentative.* The earlier in the process, the more tentative the name will be. Besides, there will always be opportunities to understudy. As I mentioned in Chapter 1, understudying is one of the most valuable of career-building opportunities. If you see an actor similar in age and type to yourself listed as a cast member for a future production that is scheduled to start rehearsal in the near future, submit your photo and resume to the casting office as a possible understudy. Be sure to include a brief cover letter making this *specific* request.

Recently, two actors told me particularly interesting stories of auditions they had gotten for themselves through this method. Both cases involved revivals of plays with major stars cast in the lead roles. Actor #1 got her audition after submitting to the casting director a photo of herself taken during a rehearsal of a proposed production of this same play—a production that had lost its funding and never got mounted. She had learned of the Broadway revival, looked up the casting director's name in the *Index,* and sent the rehearsal photo to him, suggesting herself as the star's understudy. He had her on the phone a few days later, and offered her an audition, despite the fact that she had never actually played the role.

Actor #2 *unintentionally* submitted herself by sending a fan letter to the star of another revival that had already opened. She had intended simply to congratulate the star on her outstanding performance. She sent no photo and resume with her letter, and asked for nothing. However, in the course of her letter, she told the star that she herself had recently played the same role in a showcase production. She made a couple of brief but intelligent comments regarding the similarity of their interpretations, and signed off. Within a few days, the casting director of the play called her and told her that the show's star had given her the letter, because they were in the process of casting an understudy for the role. She was asked to audition.

The common factor in both of these cases was that the actors had given specific information (albeit inadvertently in case #2), *that touched upon the needs of the casting directors.* Note especially in case #2, where the actor did not send her photo and resume, no one said, "Who is this person? Is she a member of Equity? [In fact, she was not.] What kind of credentials does she have? Does she have an agent? Did she go to Yale or Juilliard? So what if she did a *showcase* production of this play!" No. They said, "She's done this role, let's get her in here!"

Actor #1 had only rehearsed the role, and Actor #2 had performed her role in a non-paying showcase production, and yet communicating this information to the right people brought each of them top-level auditions from two very formidable casting directors. This direct approach will not always result in an audition, but remember, most submissions made by agents do not result in an audition either.

The above stories illustrate the value in giving a casting director a *reason* to grant you an audition, which is often what an agent does. Such occurrences are not rare. In fact, they are very common, especially in the theater. This very week I met an actor who told me she had just been called in to meet with a major film and theater casting director, not for understudy but to read for a supporting role in a new Broadway revival starring two of the biggest stars in the entertainment industry. Agentless, she had submitted herself for a specific role for which she felt suited. Obviously, the casting director was in agreement. I would like to point out that the actor in this case was middle-aged, and her credits rather modest. And unlike the actors in the previous stories, she had neither rehearsed nor played the role for which she was granted an audition. However, she was *aware* and she was *specific*.

You will notice in some cases in the *Theatrical Index* that the name of a casting director for a *future* production will not yet be listed. *If*, and I stress *if*, you have a reason to believe that there may be a role for which you are suited—as in the above case—telephone the office of the play's producer (the number will be listed), and ask who the casting director will be. The name that is underlined is the producer's. If they have hired a casting director, they will tell you who it is.

Knowing that the very thought of telephoning a producer's office strikes fear and doubt into the hearts of most actors, we must consider why. The reason that actors have so much difficulty (and understandably so) making telephone calls is that in most cases, the actor is either requesting an interview, an audition, or at times, even a job. It becomes quite another matter when one is seeking a simple bit of information. To stay on top of this kind of advice I offer, I periodically call the offices of producers and casting directors—without giving my name—just to gather information—and I always get the information I am seeking. A couple of recent examples: A listing in the *Index* detailed an upcoming Broadway production, which was based on a novel. Seeing no name listed as the casting director of the production, I telephoned the office of the play's producer and asked who would be doing the casting. "Are you an actor?" I was asked. This was a first. To see if it would make a difference of any kind, I said that I was. I was asked to hold on, and a few moments later, the voice returned. The producer would be casting it himself, I was told. I thanked the voice and prepared to hang up. "Do we have your photo and resume?" I was asked. "No," I said. "Well, get one over to our office at 1515 Broadway, suite such and such right away, and we'll take a look at it. Casting starts in about a week." Not bad.

I next called the office of the producer of a proposed revival of a classic. Again, I inquired about the casting personnel. The voice at this producer's office told me that she did not know if a casting director had yet been hired, but if I would leave my name and telephone number, the producer would get back to me. Two days later, there was another voice, this time the producer herself (whom I do not know, nor does she know me) on my answering machine. She identified herself, and told me that from my message she assumed I was an actor. She said that she just hired a casting director last week, and told me who it was. A "biggie." She went on to tell me that auditions would start in about four months, and that I should get in touch with her a little closer to that time if I wished to audition. With that, she thanked me for my interest in her show and said goodbye.

Tell most actors that you can call the producer of a Broadway production, and the producer might actually call you back, and they'd never believe it. Why did I get such a good-natured response from these people? Mainly, of course, because I was making a simple request for information. In the case where the producer called me back, I established myself in her mind as being in a league with a very small percentage of actors by a) knowing what was going on so far in advance, and b) knowing how to find the information I was seeking.

The question now is, what to do with this information? In the case of the first production, where it was suggested that I send directly to the producer, as casting was imminent, I would send the following typed letter to the producer:

Dear Mr. Harris:

Per my conversation with your office today, I am submitting my photo and resume for your upcoming production of *American Dreamer.*

As you can see by my resume, I have performed in several plays by Tennessee Williams and am strongly skilled in the Southern dialect that will be required for the production.

I am especially interested in the role of Joe, but will be pleased to audition for any role or understudy for which you feel I am suited.

Thank you.

Sincerely,

Brian O'Neil

Remember, *Theatrical Index* told me this play was based on a novel, hence my knowledge of the characters, and the required dialect. I mentioned my background in Williams. *Specificity* and *reason.*

In the case where my call had been returned by the producer of the proposed revival of the classic, I would immediately send *two* letters, along with my photo and resume. The first letter, of course, would go to the producer herself. It would look like this:

Dear Ms. Reynolds:

Just a brief note, along with my photo and resume, to thank you for returning my call regarding your upcoming Broadway production of *Othello.* With a strong background in the classics, I am especially interested in auditioning for Roderigo, but would be eager to read for any role or understudy for which you may feel I am suited. As you suggested, I will be in touch with you in about four months.

Thank you.

Sincerely,

Brian O'Neil

I would send the *second* letter to the play's casting director, whose name, of course, had been given to me by the producer. It would go like this:

Dear Mr. Fields:

Jane Reynolds, the producer of next season's Broadway production of *Othello,* has told me that you will be the play's casting director. I am enclosing my photo and resume and would like to be considered for the role of Roderigo, or for any role or understudy for which you may feel I am suited.

Thank you.

Sincerely,

Brian O'Neil

Important: In this letter I say that "Jane Reynolds . . . has told me . . ." which is, of course, true. She not only told me, but she called me and told me. However, I did not say, "Jane Reynolds *suggested* I send you a photograph," which might be interpreted as a referral. I am only using the name as an attention getter, which is what a good cover letter is all about. It is highly unlikely that very many letters crossing the desk of this casting director will begin with the mention of the name of the producer who had just hired him to cast her upcoming Broadway production.

My follow-up strategy in the above case would be to report any progress of consequence (jobs, *important* call-backs, etc.) to both the producer and the casting director between the time of my first writing and the time of casting, in hopes of getting on the "to be seen" list. If I were unable to enlist an agent to help me secure an audition—and I certainly would try—I would call the producer's office again (in about "four months" in her words), and request an audition. By this time, I would be confident that, having pumped positive information and progress reports to her, I might make her "list." If my attempts to get an audition failed, I would attend the EPA—if I were an

Equity member. But by covering myself with both the producer, who has specifically said to get back in touch, as well as with the casting director, my chances of being seen would increase.

Other times when I feel the actor should always "cover" himself is when there is a role for which he feels suited in a current, long-running production. I always advise submitting a photo and resume to the casting director of this production, specifying the role you are interested in. Currently running Broadway productions—along with the casting director's names—will be listed in *Theatrical Index* under the heading "Currently on the Boards." Current off-Broadway casting information is listed under the heading "Current Off-Broadway Attractions." Casts, including understudies, usually undergo many changes in the course of a long run, and it is not at all uncommon for casting directors to call in actors from this method of self-submission. If the production is a big hit, there will probably also be a national tour in the works. As the run continues, be sure to report *important* career progress, and send flyers to invite the casting director to see any work in which you feel you excel. Be sure the overall quality of the production you are in is good before you invite casting personnel to see it. Always be sure to mention the name of the production and the specific role you are interested in each time you correspond! Remember, you are trying to tap into a specific need of theirs—being general is not an effective approach.

In time, you will undoubtedly see in *Theatrical Index* that the casting director with whom you are staying in touch will be casting another project for which you may feel you are suited! In such a case, your photo postcard—or note—might say something like this:

Dear Ms. Roberts:

Just returned from playing Tom at South Shore Rep's *The Glass Menagerie.* Classically trained and experienced in plays with verse and heightened language—from Shakespeare to Stoppard—I would welcome the opportunity to audition for Mercutio in Olney Stage's upcoming production of *Romeo and Juliet.*

Thanks!

My best,

Brian O'Neil

Will the above approach work all the time? No! *Most* of the time? Probably not. Sometimes? Yes. The point isn't how often it will "work." The point is that this is what you *must* do. How often it will work will depend on several factors: the availability of the role, whether the casting director agrees that you are suited for it, the extent of your professional background, how strongly you tap into the needs of the casting director, and your timing. Of course, none of this is to say that you don't want or need an agent. You do! But "covering" yourself every time you see a long-running play that has a role you might be right for is not an overwhelming task. If only it were! But, sadly, there are not so many opportunities available that you can afford to let one good one slip past.

American Theatre Magazine

For an ongoing calendar-style overview of regional theater productions, I suggest getting *American Theatre* magazine. Published ten times a year (see Appendix E for address), *American Theatre* is available at theater bookstores, by subscription, and at selected newsstands throughout the United States. Among its many fine features, each issue of *American Theatre* gives a superb capsule look at what's happening at approximately two hundred regional theaters in all fifty states. Its October "season preview" issue lists the specific plays and directors for the entire season at each of these theaters. Be sure to get this issue especially, and save it.

The Regional Theatre Directory

For a remarkably well-researched guide to the hiring and casting procedures used by well over four hundred Equity and non-Equity regional and dinner theaters throughout the United States, I highly recommend *The Regional Theatre Directory*. Edited and published annually by Theatre Directories, a project of American Theatre Works, Inc., the *Directory* is available at theater bookstores in New York and Los Angeles, and by mail or phone as well (see Appendix E).

All theaters listed in the *Directory* include the names of administrative staff, the size of the theater, its history and artistic philosophy, and how casting is conducted and by whom. Casting information is listed under the heading of "Performers," and is included with each theater listed. Also included are the titles of plays produced in the past season and, where available, titles of productions proposed for the theater's *upcoming* season. An examination of the *Directory* will show that many theaters throughout the country routinely engage the services of a casting director in a large city, most commonly New York. For this reason, I suggest that the New York actor scrutinize the *Directory* and draw up a list of which casting directors regularly cast for theater companies out of town. And where they are indicated, jot down names of these theaters' proposed *future* productions, and list them along with the name of the theater, and the New York casting director. For the actor seeking work in regional theater, becoming aware of upcoming productions and who will be casting them, can only help. In *The Regional Theatre Directory*'s appendices, there is a section further detailing resourceful tips and strategies for actors, directors, and others in pursuit of work in regional theater.

In addition to the information provided for "out-of-town" theaters, actors and other theater artists living in such large cities as Los Angeles, Chicago, and New York especially—where there are so many theaters—should avail themselves of the wealth of information in the *Directory* pertaining to well-known, and lesser well-known, theaters in these cities. In big cities, we often tend to think of "regional" theater as being "out-of-town," which it usually is. But wherever we live, to those who do not also live there, we are "out-of-town," and in some other "region." (We New Yorkers tend to be especially guilty on this score—to us, everywhere but New York is definitely "out-of-town"!) For this reason, I find the superb city listings to be a surprise to most actors.

Time Out New York and *L.A. Weekly*

The actor who is a resident of any large city should fully research the "local" theater scene and create his own audition opportunities. Check your local weekly publications. In New York, I find *Time Out New York* very thorough in its theater listings. It is the off-off-Broadway productions that usually fall under the general term "showcases," and *Time Out* lists them in great detail. Current productions as well as performance schedules, and even subway directions are published. In Los Angeles, *L.A. Weekly* has a good rundown of the goings-on at 99-seat theaters, the Los Angeles counterpart of New York's "Equity-approved showcases." (See Appendix E.) These weekly periodicals give performance information that will assist you in researching theaters at which you might like to work. Do as much homework as you can to see which theaters regularly do the kinds of plays that interest you. Become aware of which theaters get reviewed in the press, as well as the theaters you have heard good things about. Make a list of these theaters. Then, do an Internet search to see which of these theaters have websites. Be sure to read the mission statement or artistic philosophy of each theater of interest. Look up the name of the artistic director or casting contact. This will take time and research but you will have a list of all the theaters where *you* would like to work. This will be the beginning of your own independent plan to create audition opportunities for yourself. From my own experience, this method is much more fun, and far more satisfying than waiting for the latest issue of the trade papers and finding yourself hoping "there's something this week." The actor/victim syndrome strikes again!

After assembling your list of theaters that have aroused your interest, the next step is to *start seeing work at these theaters.* This should be scheduled as your budget allows. The going ticket price at these "showcase"-type theaters is reasonable, so try to set up a regular schedule of attendance at "your" theaters.

When you attend a performance at one of these theaters, size up the situation. See if you can pick up a brochure that tells you about future productions. This information may also be listed in the program and online, if no brochure is available. Is this an actual theater company, or do different groups book the theater for their own productions? The more information you have, the easier it will be to request an audition.

When you have enjoyed a production at a specific theater, on the following day assemble a photo, resume, and cover letter addressed to the casting contact, stating that you saw the production, and specifically what you liked about it. State also that you would like the opportunity to audition, and that you will contact them again in the near future. Send it off. To the actor in New York, especially, I *always* recommend dropping it off in person. I am a great believer in "showing up." It is the rare place that will not accept a hand-delivered envelope addressed to a specific individual!

As an actor, my own implementation of this direct approach to the theaters was haphazard and disorganized, but still it paid off. I was cast in my first play in New York after tearing out the off-Broadway listings in the back of *New York* magazine and dropping off my photo and resume at all the theaters listed. At one, The Perry Street Theatre, my timing happened to be perfect. The person seated at the desk was about to direct a play. She told me I was right for one of the roles and granted me an audition on the spot. Remember, I did not ask for anything in person. I was merely there to drop off my photo and resume. My request for an audition was contained within the enclosed letter. At another, the Irish Arts Center, I was also lucky (luck of the Irish?). Figuring that I had to *look* like something they might be able to use there, I trudged over one snowy morning, manila envelope in hand. The person to whom I gave it turned out to be the theater's main director. I suppose there was something about my "Abe Lincoln" approach that impressed him. He told me he was just leaving, but would I like to join him for coffee across the street? Indeed, I would. By the time my informal "interview" was over, I was told that there would be something for me to read for before long. And there was. (By the way, he paid for the coffee, too.)

Was this kind of reception the norm? Hell, no! This kind of immediate response was the *exception.* The business of acting is all about exceptions. Successful actors are exceptions, rare exceptions! Getting the part is the exception! I went to over twenty theaters, and two expressed an immediate interest. Pretty good odds for "showing up." I especially recommend this method to the beginning actor. In my own case, my credits consisted only of college productions, but it was enough to get me a professional start.

After you have seen a play at a theater company that you have liked, and you have dropped off or mailed your photo and resume, you will need to follow up. Telephone in a week, and request an audition. If the answer is no, it will usually mean, "No, for now." You will need to follow up further. How? Progress reports, by mail. You may even decide to wait before making the first phone call, by keeping up your written correspondence. If that is more comfortable, then by all means do it. In a short time, they will start to become aware of who you are. Very few actors persist at this "grassroots" level.

When you are cast in something, somewhere, invite the others you are approaching, especially if you can get complimentary tickets. If you cannot, and your budget is tight, perhaps invite the one or two you would especially like to see your work. In any case, you are inviting them *as your guest,* so make sure you provide the tickets at no expense to them. Even if they cannot attend, they are becoming aware of your career progress. And of course, you can always report the "almosts"— call-backs for quality theater productions. The higher the level of the production, the stronger the impression. It stands to reason that a small theater company in search of talented actors might be interested in meeting an actor who "almost" got a Broadway, off-Broadway, or regional theater contract. Perhaps most important of all, *keep going back to see the productions at any theater you are targeting.*

Recently, two actors came to see me, separately, but in the

same dilemma. Having found acting opportunities hard to come by, each had the brave spirit to have founded their own theater companies. The good news was that both theater companies were thriving, but both actors had become so bogged down in the administrative work at their theaters that they had no time to act. This had not been in the plans at all! Both of them told me that they wanted to step outside their theaters, explore a little bit, and get involved in productions where their performances would be their only responsibilities. What to do? I suggested doing some research and follow-up at other theaters, along the lines of the above. After outlining the plan, I said this to each: "You cast and direct plays at your own theater. If you were approached by an actor in the manner I am suggesting, would you ask that actor to audition for you?" In both cases, the answer was an emphatic "Yes!" Both of them stressed that they would be especially interested in auditioning the actor who stayed in touch with them, and who regularly came to see productions at their theaters. People, especially in *business,* are generally more willing to support the endeavors of those who support theirs. Therefore, when you continue to see the productions at a particular theater, be sure to let the person you are contacting know that you have returned to see their latest production. Do this by dropping them a line and telling them succinctly and specifically what you liked about it. Be sincere. It should go without saying that if you find the work at any theater to be poor, or consistently substandard, move on and explore new territory.

Recently, an actor, new to the business, met with me, and from the listings in *Time Out New York* and the "NYC Area" section of the *Regional Theatre Directory,* we drew up a list of small theater companies that matched his strengths and interests. I sent him out with specific instructions to follow the "plan" as outlined above. He reported back that every theater at which he stopped in person accepted his initial correspondence. In the short few weeks that had elapsed, two theaters had already called him in, and he was making promising headway at a few others.

FILM

While a long-range overview of film production is recommended for any actor pursuing work in this area of the industry, major studio film auditions are, in general, far less accessible than theater auditions. Even represented, the unknown actor often has a difficult time getting seen for sizable roles in major film productions. Why? By and large, the film industry is looking for recognizable names to fill these leading and supporting roles in order to help attract audiences. Even when the unknown actor is granted the opportunity to read for such a role, it will usually be awarded to someone who has more visibility, and is better known to the moviegoing public. Look at the movie section in a daily newspaper, and you will see that the great majority of the actors' names listed are the same names you have been seeing in films for at least the past few years, if not longer. To be sure, new actors penetrate this highly competitive circle, but in most cases, the process has taken place more slowly than it might appear. With the exception of extremely young actors—who in some cases are the offspring of famous parents—or the occasional superstar from the music industry, most new faces in film belong to one of two "breeds" of actors.

First, there are those who have recently made a big splash in the New York theater, or, as has been the trend in the past decade, there are those who are "crossing over" from successful careers in prime-time or comedy television. Previously a rare occurrence, it is now very common to see the star of a hit television series also starring in theatrically released motion pictures at the very same time. This is due in large part to the advent of pay television and the video/DVD rental phenomenon, which has caused the public's perception of the difference between film and television to narrow. A kind of "blending" has taken place, and television stars have become potential "box-office." Today, to be the star of a hit television series frequently means being offered a starring role in a feature film as well.

The Hollywood Reporter (HollywoodReporter.com) and The Internet Movie Database Pro (IMDbPro.com)

For a thorough listing of current and *future* projects, my first choice is *The Hollywood Reporter* (HollywoodReporter.com). At this time, only the online version of the *Reporter* offers film production "charts." These charts list films already in production and give a rundown of each film's shooting locations, producer, director, screenwriter, stars, and in most cases, the film production company's address, phone number, and the name of the production's casting director. Following the listing of films already in production, *The Reporter* gives a lengthy list of films scheduled for *future* production, again detailing the film's shoot locations, stars (if set), producer, director, screenwriter, casting director, and production company. *Future and pre-production films listed on* The Reporter's *website are frequently listed up to six months in advance.* While most film production offices and shooting locations will be listed as being in Los

Angeles, the New York actor should keep an eye peeled for various films scheduled to shoot in New York.

Sometimes New York is listed as one of the shooting locations, but only a Los Angeles production company or casting contact is listed. To learn if casting will be done in New York as well as in Los Angeles, and who will be doing it, call the phone number listed and announce that you are calling from New York to inquire who will be handling the New York casting for a particular film. I do this quite regularly, and as is the case with theater, I always get the information I am seeking.

Once again, I direct the actor to IMDbPro.com, which contains a multitude of information regarding upcoming film and television productions. (IMDbPro also offers links to select *Hollywood Reporter* articles.) When visiting IMDbPro to research a *specific* film or television production, type the name of the film or television production (the movie or show title) into the site's search box. Once you have navigated to the film's or television show's page, click on "Full Credits" on the left in order to find the name of that production's *casting director.* A subscription to both HollywoodReporter.com and IMDbPro.com will keep the film and television actor more in the know than has ever before been possible.

Since the film and prime-time television industries are so highly competitive, in most cases it will be necessary for the actor to have representation in order to be considered for principal roles in films. However, film casting directors have certainly been known to call in actors from self-submissions. Anyone can submit a photo, resume, and cover letter to a film casting director in the very same manner one submits to a casting director for stage productions.

As difficult as the film (and prime-time television) industry is to penetrate, opportunities have expanded all over the country in less competitive markets than Los Angeles and New York. In the next chapter, we will examine existing opportunities for the beginner—as well as for the more professionally seasoned actor—on the regional and local scene: in theater and film, as well as in the television, commercial, and industrial markets.

8

The Local Scene

Exploring the local scene can be of great benefit to any actor, prior to making the leap to a highly competitive market, such as Los Angeles or New York. In fact, in recent years, many actors have abandoned both meccas, and sought greener pastures in various other cities throughout the United States. Although Los Angeles remains the capital of film and television production, and New York still reigns in commercial theater and television commercial production, countless millions of dollars are spent annually in film, television, stage, commercial, and corporate (industrial) production across the country. As actors migrated to such cities as Miami, Chicago, Seattle, and San Francisco, new talent agencies opened, and more and more actors have joined the unions in cities other than New York and Los Angeles. One or more of the talent unions now have offices in such cities as Boston, Chicago, Dallas, Miami, Minneapolis/St. Paul, Washington, D.C., Phoenix, Atlanta, Cleveland,

Honolulu, Nashville, Louisville, Detroit, Denver, St. Louis, and New Orleans. In addition, there are now union-franchised talent agencies in over half the states in the United States.

While talent agencies in some large cities (Los Angeles, Dallas, and Seattle among them) work with actors on a signed, exclusive basis only, agencies in most cities will work on a freelance basis.

Since most of the earnings made by actors come from employment in film, television, commercials, radio, and industrials, talent agencies around the country are more likely to represent actors in these areas of the industry than to represent them for employment in the theater.

Many states, especially southern ones, are known as "right to work" states. A "right to work" state allows an individual to accept employment without union membership becoming mandatory. Therefore, the local actor who is not yet a member of the unions would be wise to explore all performance opportunities in film, commercials, television, radio, and industrials on the local scene.

Any professional actor will need an arsenal of photos and resumes, but how does the local newcomer know where to find a good photographer? Some of the larger cities in the U.S. have good theater-oriented publications that contain advertisements for professional photographers. In areas where there are no publications of this nature, either contact a local casting office, the office of the nearest franchised talent agency, or the nearest branch of one of the talent unions. Any of these listed offices can help you to find a photographer. Once photos are taken, you will need a resume. Follow the same guidelines, wherever possible, as outlined in Chapter 2. Check with local talent agencies to see what their registration procedures are. No reputable representative asks for money up front. Agents get paid after their actors get work. If there are no talent agencies in your area, contact local advertising agencies and television production companies, which can be found through an Internet search. Ask these companies if you can submit your photo and resume to them.

For professional theater employment on the local scene, I again recommend the use of periodicals as a guideline to Internet research of theaters in your area—small towns and big cities as well. Become aware of the current, or better yet, upcoming season at each theater of interest. Many websites will list hiring procedures and some will tell you the best time of year to make contact. Keep a list of these theaters (assuming that there are some) as well as when "general" auditions are held, if it is a theater's policy to conduct them. If information is not provided as to whom one should send one's photo and resume, either email or call the theater and request the name of the approriate person. For the aspiring professional actor who is planning a move to Los Angeles, or New York especially, prior stage experience is appreciated by both agents and casting directors. Many college and regional theaters throughout the country offer prestigious full-training theater programs, as well as individual classes in all aspects of the performing arts. All of this will be good for the craft—and good for the resume, too.

In some cases, colleges are connected with regional theaters, and afford performing opportunities to students. Even a very small role at a quality regional theater looks good on the resume of the professional newcomer. To the aspiring professional actor who is a student in close proximity to a good regional theater, I suggest enlisting the aid of a theater department faculty member to invite the casting personnel from the theater to attend especially top-notch school productions. If no help is forthcoming from the faculty—you guessed it—invite them yourself.

Many colleges and universities with film departments regularly seek actors for student films. These opportunities provide excellent on-camera experience, as well as the beginnings of a demo. Check with these institutions regarding casting procedures. In addition to opportunities in university film productions, many states have established film commissions, partly to explore the economic benefits of bringing film production into the state. At the time of this writing, the southwest is holding steady, thanks in large part to former Texas governor Ann Richards. Florida, too, with Universal and Disney/MGM Studios, as well as the northwest region of the country all show film and television employment available. Despite this, most leading and supporting roles in major films and television series are cast out of Los Angeles or New York. Remember, *The Hollywood Reporter* lists *shooting locations,* as well as the proposed start date of upcoming film productions. Just as the New York actor can call Los Angeles to check on the East Coast casting contact for a specific film, so can any actor around the country make the same call or send an email to ascertain casting information about a project that will be shot locally.

Remember that in most cases, the address of the film production company and/or the casting contact will be listed. Send a photo and resume, along with a brief cover letter letting the casting personnel know that you are an actor living in the region where the film will be shot and would like to work if local talent will be used. Your state film commission, if you have one, can also apprise you of upcoming local film productions. The film commission can usually be reached through your state's Department of Commerce, or Department of Economic Development. In addition, many large cities have an AFTRA/SAG hotline, which can also help to keep the local actor abreast of potential film and television opportunities. Relocating to larger markets, such as New York or Los Angeles, accompanied by a demo of film, television, on-camera commercial, or voice-over spots that have aired, will greatly increase your chances of obtaining interviews with representatives in both these cities.

9

Reflections on Personal Management

"What do you think of personal managers?" is a question I am asked almost daily by actors. While I am amused by the generality of the question, as it presumes that all personal managers are of equal caliber and repute, the question is not unlike asking, "What do you think of people?"

As with every occupation, there are personal managers who are outstanding, and those who are not. Since no one ever asks, "What do you think of agents?" I assume that the role of the personal manager is not clear to most actors, nor perceived to be as vital. Ask an actor the difference between a talent agent and a personal manager, and most will respond, "An agent takes a ten percent commission, and a personal manager takes more." And while this is often the case, it falls far short of defining the difference—legal or functional—between the two.

Let's first take a look at the difference from a legal standpoint. Talent agencies in both New York and California are required by law to be licensed as employment agencies in order to solicit employment for others. In addition, talent agencies must be franchised by the talent unions in order to solicit employment for union members and negotiate monies for them. Upon "booking" an actor into an employment situation, the talent agency is then allowed to take a commission of ten percent on monies earned from this employment. As I mentioned in Chapter 6, the contracts offered to actors by union-franchised talent agencies are contracts that have been drawn up by the unions themselves. Therefore, these contracts and their provisions lean largely in favor of the *actor*.

No such regulations from either the state or the talent unions confine the personal manager. However, a personal manager is not licensed to seek or procure employment for his client. This is, perhaps, the most basic difference between a talent agent and a personal manager. In the New York business laws that regulate the seeking of employment for others, there is a slight "loophole," however, that allows that the personal manager's efforts on behalf of the client may involve the "incidental" procuring of employment. Since the extent of precisely what constitutes "incidental" employment is vague, most reputable personal managers in New York keep it minimal, or they risk being charged with illegally engaging in licensed trade.

For all practical purposes, then, the talent agent seeks employment for his client, and it is frowned upon for the personal manager to do so—at least in a direct fashion. What, then, does a personal manager do? In general, the personal manager oversees all aspects of the performer's career. Depending on the career level of the performer being represented, and the specifics of the personal management contract, personal managers perform a host of services. Most personal management contracts contain the significant wording, "advice, guidance, and council," within the first few paragraphs. What often follows is a list of areas in which the personal manager agrees to perform the duties of giving "advice, guidance, and council." These areas frequently include the selection of proper material for performance, advice concerning contracts and the terms of business engagements, as well as the all-important selection of other necessary personnel to help further the career of the performer. This would, of course, include the selection of the right talent agent or agents with whom the personal manager would work on behalf of his client.

It is this duty that, in my view, is amongst the more important of functions that the personal manager can provide for the actor who lacks talent agency representation.* Since the personal manager is not authorized to "book" the client into an employment situation, one needs to know that a prospective personal manager is well connected with quality talent (booking) agencies who can provide employment opportunities. The most common "employment opportunities" in our business are, of course, auditions. It is in this area specifically that the personal manager can be of great value to the professional newcomer. In New York, the client of such a personal manager can potentially benefit from the services provided by numerous talent agencies—provided the personal manager is well-connected with these talent agencies. In such situations, the actor then has access to more audition opportunities than a single talent agency may be able to furnish. Since different talent agents have different strengths—as well as different professional contacts—a truly well-managed actor can be directed to

---

* Actors who achieve a certain level of success are often approached by or seek personal management representation. In such cases, the actor already has talent agency representation, but may also require the expertise of high-level personal management to expand, organize, or supervise various career activities.

the various talent agents who coincide with his own strengths and talents.

I had working relationships with over twenty different talent agencies when I was in personal management in New York City. These talent agencies would call a number of times each day seeking specific actors or accepting clients I would suggest for each new breakdown they received. In addition to permitting agents to represent clients—by "clearing" them for specific projects in the same way that an agent "clears" an actor who is not signed to him—I had various other responsibilities as a personal manager. I coached clients for upcoming auditions, taught them on-camera commercial audition technique, and provided other services that talent agents have little time, and are not compensated, to render. These services included giving advice on proper wardrobe, audition material, detailed explanations of necessary business procedures, as well as giving extensive personal and professional support, often referred to by the minimizing term, "hand-holding." Yet there is another underrated and ongoing labor on the part of a competent and thorough personal manager. While it is true that the personal manager is not legally authorized to procure employment for his client, he is well within his legal rights and duties to hound the living hell out of a licensed talent agent who is representing the personal manager's client on a specific project. If the client of the personal manager has been "cleared" by an agent or is "signed" with said agent, an effective personal manager will see that the agent either subsequently secures an audition for the client, or furnishes the personal manager with a legitimate reason as to *why* the client will not be granted an audition. This can get on the nerves of even the most patient of talent agents, but *follow-up,* so often the actor's downfall, is a very necessary element for the success of any acting career. Therefore, follow-up is a priceless service provided by a good personal manager. Once an actor is offered a job, the personal manager uses his business expertise to advise the talent agent—who will then negotiate acceptable terms for the engagement—another valuable service on the part of quality personal management.

The above—effective follow-up and expert negotiating skills—may be of special interest to the California actor, who as I mentioned in Chapter 6 will be *signed* to only *one* talent agency (or in some cases two, if the actor is signed to a separate agency that specializes in television commercials). Remember, the practice of working through several talent agencies is not implemented in Los Angeles, as it is in New York—irrespective of personal management.

These are some of the services provided by a personal manager. To repeat, personal management contracts, unlike union-franchised talent agency contracts—which are standard—vary according to the scope of professional duties that the personal manager wishes to undertake. Also, the services provided will often depend upon the career level of the client being represented. One actor I know is represented by a personal management firm in Los Angeles, almost all of whose clients make a million dollars or more annually. The services provided by this firm are extremely broad-ranging from top-level business negotiations to picking up the star's mother at the airport.

The price of these extra services provided by personal management is the payment of two commissions: the ten percent commission the actor pays to the talent agency and the other to the personal manager. Commission rates to personal managers vary, as there is no regulated maximum, but most take a minimum of ten percent of the actor's gross earnings. Some personal management contracts have an escalation clause, whereby commissions increase as the client's earnings increase.

In addition to a second (and maybe higher) commission, the duration of the personal management contract is, in most cases, longer than that of the talent agency contract. First-time personal management contracts are often for a period of five years—the initial period being three years, followed by a two-year option, often renewable if the personal manager *alone* so desires. While no "out" clause is provided in a personal management contract, talent agency contracts are usually quite easily dissoluble if the actor is not obtaining employment. The closest thing to the "out" clause offered in personal management contracts is a "cure" clause, by which the performer may notify the personal manager in writing of the default of obligations. The personal manager then has a period of time (as stated in the contract) to remedy such defaults if, in fact, they exist. And while talent agency contracts cover only the areas of theater, film, television, commercials, and radio—all areas under the jurisdiction of the talent unions—personal management contracts are more inclusive in scope. While being represented in every area of the entertainment industry is at times negotiable, the personal management contract usually includes, as a matter of course, such areas as recording, personal appearances, publishing, and modeling. Also, talent agency contracts are for representation of the actor in *one* city—most commonly New York or Los Angeles—which is the reason many agencies have offices on both coasts. Personal management contracts, however, usually contain the phrase "throughout the world."

It is not my intention to sway the actor to *or* from the notion of seeking personal management, only to outline some essential differences, and to illustrate how agents and personal managers work in relationship with each other. Since personal management representation is not regulated or investigated in the way that talent agency representation is, it *is* my intention to propose some guidelines for the actor who is considering the possibility of personal management, and who is offered a contract by a personal manager. At the outset, I must point out that not unlike talent agency representation, no legitimate personal manager asks for money up front from a prospective client. A talent representative only makes money *after* a client gets work.

If you are offered a personal management contract, be certain to ask any and all questions you have regarding the contract itself. Consult an attorney. Ask the personal manager for any clarification you need concerning the specific duties the personal manager will undertake in your behalf.

Also ask a prospective personal manager his long-range view for your career. Remember that a personal management contract is usually a long-term commitment. In which area or areas of the industry does the personal manager see you working—and, hopefully, flourishing? It is of utmost importance that you and a prospective personal manager see your career possibilities in the same light.

Prior to a meeting with a personal manager, research the manager—as you would an agent—on IMDbPro.com and ascertain the following: How many clients does the personal manager represent? Does he represent any clients whose careers you might be familiar with? How many clients are at approximately the same career level as yourself? Since the duties of the personal manager are broader in scope than those of the agent, ideally the personal manager represents fewer clients than the talent agent. Does the personal manager handle six clients or twenty-six? In learning the number of clients represented by the personal manager and assessing the career levels with which the personal manager is currently dealing, you can get a better sense of how much time and attention might be allotted to you and your career needs.

Ask what actions on the part of the personal manager you can expect *immediately upon signing.* If you lack talent agency representation, will you be introduced right away to the talent agents with whom the personal manager has working relationships? There are times when a personal manager will have a very legitimate reason not to introduce you to any agents immediately—you may be completing an acting program, or even beginning an on-camera commercial technique class at the time of your signing with the personal manager. The manager may want to wait until this training is complete. Also, many managers utilize the vague "incidental bookings" situation to help a client get some manner of employment as a way of enticing prospective talent agents. These are all reasons why a personal manager may delay introductions to agents. The point is that you have a right to know a prospective personal manager's planned course of action for you. And the personal manager should be happy to share this information with you. *Vagueness or reluctance on the part of the personal manager to discuss any of these things with you should be a warning signal.*

Ask how many talent agencies the personal manager has working relationships with. And which talent agencies are they? Does he work with one or two agencies? Or is it ten or twelve? This is also of critical importance for a couple of reasons. I have known New York actors to sign with a manager only to later discover that the personal manager has working relationships with two talent agencies—the same two with which the actor was already freelancing. No new contacts there. This point is important, as it can give you a sense of the degree of possible options and prospects you will have with regard to talent agency representation in conjunction with the personal manager. *Reluctance to discuss which talent agencies the personal manager has working relationships with should be another warning signal.*

Does the personal manager subscribe to Breakdown Services? You will want to know if he receives this detailed, daily outline of projects being cast for theater, film, and television. Some personal managers rely on what is sometimes a rather sketchy rundown of information from talent agents pertaining to the role and project for which you are auditioning. Equally important, some talent agents understandably do not seek to represent the clients of personal managers on projects that are low-paying. These projects often appear on Breakdown Services, and it would be to your advantage if your personal manager is aware of them. Often these projects are stage productions, and while the pay may be low, they may well be artistically desirable, as well as career-advancing. I don't think it's an absolute necessity that the personal manager be a subscriber to Breakdown Services—its availability to personal managers is limited—provided his relationships with agents are strong and thorough. However, it certainly helps, and you will want to know whether or not a prospective personal manager has access to this information.

One last question—this is one to ask yourself: Do you trust and like this person? The issue of trust is probably self-evident, as you will be relying on your personal manager for guidance, support, and career direction. You will presume that your personal manager is acting in your best interest at all times. You will allow that payment for your services as a performing artist will go to your manager, before it goes to you. And while every good and close relationship has its bumpy moments, for the personal manager/performing artist relationship to thrive, both parties must have a healthy and mutual respect. Discussions of the pros and cons, pluses and minuses of personal management are never ending. Yet the word *personal* is critical in the term *personal management,* and the need, desire, or inclination to seek it, and with whom, is a *personal,* as well as a professional decision. A final thought: I am of the opinion that many of the finest personal managers are themselves former talent agents who have since chosen to "specialize"—so to speak.

10

Q&A

Q: You have a very strong conviction about the stage being the route to film or prime-time television for the New York actor. Why do you think this point is unclear to so many actors?

A: When an actor from the New York stage "makes the jump" to a career in film or prime-time television, very often the media plays down the actor's stage career, since it means little to the public at large, and is now dwarfed by his film or TV career. It also gives the interviewer or journalist a great "American dream" angle. It appears that the actor burst on the scene out of nowhere. Recently, an actor disagreed with what he referred to as my "theory" about the stage-to-screen process in New York. He mentioned a new "film" actor who was from New York. According to articles he had read about her, she had basically been "discovered," although she hadn't been doing any acting of note.

What these articles failed to mention—and this is my point—was that shortly before this actor had burst on the scene out of "nowhere," she had been performing leading roles at some of New York's most prominent off- and off-off-Broadway theater companies—the Signature and Primary Stages, among them. That was, as is usually the case, how the "discovery" had actually taken place. The fact is, actors are simply being cast in film and television productions from *smaller* stage venues than before.

Q: But it's a different ball game in Los Angeles?

A: Mucho different. Los Angeles is not about the theater, and New York is. Some of our biggest stars in film today *do not* come from the theater. Although they did some early stage work, Kevin Costner, Harrison Ford, and Jack Nicholson, for example, did not become known to the film industry through their careers on the stage. The same is true of many younger film stars, whose careers began as children or teens in television on the West Coast.

Q: Do you have any suggestions as to how the New York actor can create audition opportunities in the independent film market?

A: Turn back to page 118 and re-read the section regarding *The Hollywood Reporter.* Keep abreast of non-studio films that are scheduled to be shot in New York, especially those involving screenwriters and/or directors whose previous work you may have enjoyed. Some actors submit their photos and resumes to the screenwriter/director (or casting director) of the film at the film production office and are subsequently granted auditions. Due to relatively low budgets, the creative teams of these "indie" projects are often far more open to the unrepresented—and less experienced—actor than would be the case with a more mainstream "big studio" production. Some actors call the production office and ask, for example, "are there any roles available for young men (women) in their early twenties, because if so, I'd like to submit my photo and resume for your consideration." Other actors, however, simply send in their photo and resume without checking the specifics. Whatever method you choose, if you have seen and admired the screenwriter's or director's previous work, be sure to tell them so—sincerely and intelligently—in your cover letter. Not only will it genuinely be appreciated, but assuming there is a role for which you might be suited, it will also increase your chances of getting an audition. I've been delighted to see a number of actors crack the "indie" market by implementing this approach!

Q: You said earlier that of the actors working in the New York theater, only a small percentage are names from film or television. Why does it seem just the opposite?

A: A couple of reasons. The first and most obvious being that the stars are the ones whose names we recognize, and of course, if they're in a play they will be playing the leads. The second reason has to do with the negative thinking that actors are, unfortunately, often prone to: "If you're not a name in film or TV, you can't get stage work" . . . "If you didn't go to Yale or Juilliard or the MFA program at NYU" . . . "If you're not twenty-three" . . . "If you aren't signed with such and such an agency . . ." "If your parents aren't famous . . ."

  The following is an absolutely true story. I ran into an actor I know, who said to me "If you didn't go to Yale or Juilliard, you can't get an acting job. . . ." Later that week, I ran into another actor I know. He was a graduate of the Yale School of Drama. He said, "If you're not signed to one of the top five agencies, you can't get a decent audition in this town." Several days later, I ran into another actor I know, this one signed with the William Morris Agency (certainly in the top five!). He said, "If you're not in your early twenties, you can't get seen for anything these days." And so it goes. It's very understandable, and we all complain, but the actor is especially vulnerable to it, and must keep it in check, or he won't be able to go on with any sense of well-being. Our attitudes do us in long before our aptitudes do.

Q: You seem to de-emphasize the importance of the photograph. Why?

A: I only mean to de-emphasize the *over*importance of the photograph. I don't mean that it's not important. It is. However, I also feel that far too much is often made of it. Or it's another case of an excuse being handed out as a reason. Let me give you an example. Recently, an actor just out of school had her photos taken. I saw them, and while I felt they were less than ideal, the quality was good. She told me that an agent she had just met at a seminar had hated the photos and suggested that she not even use them. Based on her talent, the agent would represent her, she was told. But not with those photos. I thought the agent had been irresponsible in making that statement, especially since I suspected that this agent was not going to be working with this actor anyway. Had he been interested in representing her, I can assure you he would have dealt with the photos until such time as the actor could afford new ones. I suggested that she ignore the agent's advice, and proceed with the photos. You guessed the rest. At one of the offices where she sent her photo, she got called in, and now she has an agent. These occurrences are not rare—they happen all the time. In fact, I later learned that the agent in this story was working with another actor whom he had met at the same seminar, who did not even *have* photographs! My point should be clear. The photo issue is subjective, and should never keep the actor from taking action, unless the photos misrepresent you. An acting career is not about photographs; it is about being *out there.*

Q: From a "business" standpoint, what are the benefits of performing in regional theater?

A: Due to sheer geographics, the number of high-level professional productions being mounted at regional theaters in any given season exceeds what can be found off- and on Broadway that same season. Working in good regional theater productions *positions* an actor better for New York theater employment. Here is why. Note that when you attend a performance of a major off-Broadway (or Broadway) production, the majority of cast members have regional theater credits in their biographies. Often, it is these very credits that built their resumes and made these actors more professionally attractive to those who cast for New York. In fact, most of the casting directors of Broadway and off-Broadway productions have "regional accounts." That is, they cast productions for regional theaters as well as for New York, and therefore through their multiple casting duties encounter many of the same actors. It is also not uncommon for an actor to be appearing in a top off-Broadway or Broadway production because the *director* of said production has *previously* directed that same actor in a regional production. In other words, those who direct on and off-Broadway often direct regional theater productions as well. Regional theater is a very powerful way for an actor to make high-level contacts.

Another advantage of working in regional theater concerns *agents*. It is common for an unrepresented actor to return from a regional engagement with one or two or more appointments lined up with New York agents. Why? Simple. Often, these actors' colleagues in the cast already have representation, and their agents travel out of town to see their clients' work. (Well, the *good* ones do, anyway!) At that time, the work of an unrepresented actor can come to the agents' attention, and agents will often subsequently invite the actor to meet with them upon returning home. The irony here is that it is sometimes easier to have your work seen by an agent when you are employed in a production being done several hundred miles outside of town than it is to get an agent to come and see you in a play being performed six blocks from his office!

Last, but certainly not least: Many actors will need to put themselves "on the map," as it were, before being able to acquire representation. By this, I mean that an actor may have to land an impressive credit or two before his or her career will be of interest to an agent. Many actors have gone to a higher career level through their employment in regional theater.

For a quality look at the upcoming regional season, including names of directors, artistic directors, and casting directors, my periodical of choice is the *Season Overview* (see Appendix E), which also contains listings and websites for top off-Broadway theater companies as well.

Q: Speaking of websites, can you elaborate on some of the more valuable aspects of Internet usage for an actor?

A: Okay, here goes. As I have implied throughout the book, I believe that one of the greatest uses of the Internet for an actor (and for anyone seeking employment in any field, for that matter) is to use it as a *research tool*. Many actors go online to various casting websites, which is fine, but neither as creative nor effective as would be ideal. It is also true that through email, many actors *illegally* get their hands—and eyes—on *copyrighted* breakdowns written for the exclusive use of agents who have *paid* for those breakdowns. Though rumor persists that only the *distributor* of said illegal dispensation of copyrighted breakdowns risks a lawsuit, be aware that the *recipient* also risks legal action as well. That said, *any* breakdown (legal or not) that has been designed, drawn up, and spelled out as a *breakdown* (and this includes trade publication casting notices as well) attracts hordes of actors *all at the same time.* Therefore the "casting system" gets glutted, cluttered, and the actor typically gets more and more lost, all of which is why I have previously encouraged the (legal) *researching* of information regarding upcoming productions as far in advance as possible. In any subsequent self-submission, the actor is able to make a far better impression of himself or herself by having the *time* to construct thoughtful and compelling correspondence—to say nothing of having more *time* to prepare for any audition that may result. Therefore, I have instructed my clients to research reviews of plays that may not yet be published, but have been performed in regional theater and are being planned for a New York mounting. In doing so, they are able to ascertain whether or not there might be a role or at least a possible understudy assignment in the offing. Through legitimate research, they are then able to, in effect, create their own "breakdown." Also, if an actor is extremely passionate about being considered for a role, he or she will sometimes research legitimate *business* addresses of the true power brokers of casting, i.e., the *playwrights* and the *directors* themselves. If a playwright or a director wants you brought in for an audition, *you will be brought in.* Many of my clients—including those whose credits are minimal—have been invited to audition for high-level productions being planned by major playwrights and major directors. Research of this nature takes more work, and therefore fewer people will do it, with the result being that it is ultimately *far more effective.* Here are a couple of other ideas where Internet usage for research purposes is concerned. One approach is to determine the *location* of a particular individual whom you wish to contact. Recently, I worked with an actor who was seeking an audition for a particular play. The play was slated to be produced many months down the line. Together we did an Internet search for the director and saw that he was about to direct a different play in the *near* future at a regional theater. I suggested that the actor mail his materials (photo, resume, and highly specific cover letter) to the director in care of the regional theater the week the play was scheduled to open. (This, of course, is the week of technical and dress rehearsals and therefore the director must be present.) He did as I suggested and the director received the actor's materials and called him in when the other play was set to be cast. (He got the part, too.)

The above is a combination of the new (Internet) plus the old (postal mail), the latter allowing the actor to send a nice package that would most likely stand out and also demonstrate to the director that the actor was going the extra mile to show real interest in auditioning for this director's play.

Also, social and professional networking resources such as LinkedIn, MySpace, and Facebook can be used for research purposes, and one of the most effective uses in this regard is to try to determine a potential "commonality of people." Example: An actor whom I know had an interview scheduled with an agent who had asked him to prepare a monologue. On Facebook, the actor discovered that the agent he was about to meet was a "friend" of a casting director who had given him a specific monologue that the actor enjoyed performing. He chose *that* monologue for his audition piece for the agent. He performed it well and when the agent praised him for his performance, the actor (knowingly) said: "The monologue was chosen for me by so-and-so" (naming the casting director). The agent then said, "Oh, he and I are such great friends, blah, blah, blah!" and an enthusiastic conversation ensued between the actor and the agent. Note that the actor kept his "research" to himself and didn't say, "I saw on Facebook that you and so-and-so are friends so I chose this monologue, blah, blah, blah." In other words, he took a far more subtle approach.

The irony of all this is that we're so often led to believe that modern communication is "impersonal." Actually, it can be highly personal and therefore should be used with discretion, as the above example would demonstrate. Here are a few general tips for Internet usage and email etiquette. Since people are easier to get to than ever before, one of the main things to remember is the importance of *capturing their attention.* Therefore, the *subject* of an email is critical, and your email must contain one in the subject line. Also, be certain that where an email is concerned, the *final words* you type should be the recipient's email address, which will help to avoid the possibility of sending off any correspondence prematurely. And *always* fire back a quick thank-you to anyone who emails you with helpful and/or requested information. Last, but not least, bear in mind that anything you send can be endlessly forwarded.

Q: As an actor who has been working more and more, I sometimes now get offers for two productions that conflict in schedule. Sometimes the choice to make is pretty obvious, but other times it presents a dilemma. Any guidelines for when I'm in a quandry?

A: The next time this happens, get a sheet of paper and draw a line straight down the center. On the left-hand side, list in the following order: the title of the play, the role, the theater, the director, and the salary for offer number one. In the right-hand column, do the exact same thing for offer number two. Now go down *both* columns and place a check mark next to your preference in each individual category. When you have finished, you will see that you have placed five check marks. One column will *always* have more check marks than the other. *Now* make your decision.

Q: What are the benefits of participating in play readings that are performed at quality theaters?

A: There are a number of benefits in doing so. Artistically, of course, an actor might find himself getting in on the ground floor of a good new play! But since this book is, quite frankly, not about art, but about access and marketing, let me tell you of the value from a *business* point of view.

When an industry person looks at the theater credits on an actor's resume, it's the third column (i.e., where the actor has worked) that is read first. It is the third column that declares the status quo of an actor's career level—at least where theater is concerned. As I have already said, in New York, film and television casting personnel are very concerned with the third column of the resume of the actor who is not yet known in film and television. As such, the more prestigious the place where the actor has worked (that is, the name of the theater itself), the more the *third column* of the actor's resume is enhanced. That is, places have *reputations.* The better the place you worked at, obviously, the more impressive the resume and the better will be the perception of you. In other words, when an industry person looks at your resume, he is hoping to see something he will recognize.

Can one put play readings on one's resume? Yep. Simply put the word "reading" in parentheses next to the play's title, which will be in the first column. In doing so, you are properly qualifying the nature of the project and not implying that you appeared in a main stage production at said theater. Remember, however, that the "judgment column" is the third column, and since industry personnel will read that column first, they will see the more impressive news (the name of the theater) before they read the qualifier (reading), which will be placed next to the play's title in column one. As such, I would only consider placing readings of plays on the resume if the theater is highly respected. It stands to reason that it's easier to get in a reading at a top-notch theater than it would be to get into a main stage production at that same theater. In either case, you get to put the name of that theater in the all-important third column of your resume. I have seen many actors get in play after play at theaters that make no positive impression on the actor's resume. And I've seen other actors have doors open to them, or have a far better interview with an agent or a casting director simply because they did a reading at an important theater—and have it listed. Remember, industry people will always see more of your *resume* than they actually see of *you*. And what's "on paper" is so often what decides whether or not you get in the door. Once again, I want to stress that I would only list readings if the theater where they were presented is prestigious and known for quality work.

I would also like to emphasize that I work with many actors who are represented by top agencies, and the way I have described above is the manner in which they list readings on their resumes. Their agents have no problem with it, and neither do casting directors. If it's okay for them, it's okay for you too. All told then, readings at prestigious theaters are a good way to enhance your resume and the overall perception of you. So, please go back and re-read pages 111–117 for ideas on how to target quality theaters!

Here's another tip: A good way to keep abreast of the happenings at major theaters (specifically off-Broadway, in the case of New York), is to volunteer to usher for one performance at each of the theater's main stage productions. Simply call or email the theater and ask them about their ushering policy. The benefits? You get to see the play at no cost (which is the manner in which you will be "paid." That is, a free seat is given to you for the performance at which you ushered). Also, as a volunteer usher, you are technically on the staff of the theater for one night, and you will often have the opportunity to meet key personnel associated with the theater. It is also wise, whenever possible, to try to usher during the play's preview period. Often the playwright and the director are present, and it is possible to meet them as well. Remember, they are future contacts for you, and you can correspond with them when appropriate.

I have written elsewhere that I detest the word *networking,* and the very concept of it. However, I love the word *infiltrating,* and the very concept of *it*!

Q: Is the independent film market successfully beginning to launch many film careers in New York without benefit of prior stage visibility?

A: I'm personally very excited to see the expansion of the "indie" market, and I hope it continues, especially since getting good roles in good plays at good theaters isn't especially easy to do. The New York independent film market has certainly already launched *some* film careers, and they—along with very young actors—comprise some of the exceptions I spoke about in Chapter 1. As I mentioned, the overwhelming majority of film careers that come from New York come from the stage. As of this 2009 writing, New York film careers that come from the stage outweigh film careers that do not come from the stage at an approximate ratio of fifteen to one.

Q: It seems that lately I've seen more and more already established actors and stars turn up in independent films. Is this an accurate observation?

A: It's true that Hollywood has glommed onto the independent film market, creating in a sense two Hollywoods—and producers and potential distributors have become increasingly interested in the name value and credibility of the actors being hired. As such, agents have become more participatory in the "indie" casting process, and have accelerated the focus on nurturing young clients that they have culled from, among other places, the showcases presented by the graduates of the top academic theater training programs.

Q: Which schools are considered the "top" academic theater training programs? How much clout do they have in launching professional careers, and can you tell me more about their showcases?

A: The three most prestigious academic theater training programs, in no particular order, are: the MFA program at Yale University, the Graduate Acting Program at New York University (MFA also), and the undergraduate (BFA) program at Juilliard. There are many other popular academic training programs as well, including (again, in no particular order): Carnegie-Mellon, North Carolina School of the Arts, University of North Carolina at Chapel Hill, University of California, San Diego, Rutgers University, Temple University, University of San Diego/ Old Globe Theatre, Harvard, American Conservatory Theatre, University of Michigan, Northwestern, the National Theatre Conservatory at the Denver Center, and Brown University/Trinity Rep Consortium. (For further information, see *Directory of Theatre Training Programs,* Appendix E.)

These schools, as well as others, present showcases each spring in New York on designated afternoons or evenings (or both). The presentations consist of a series of scenes (and/or songs), and are officially known as the Actors Presentations, but are more commonly referred to as "the Leagues." Generally well attended by agents and casting directors (and awesomely so in the case of The Big Three), many actors are lured into (or back into) academia by the promise of "the big showcase" at a given program's conclusion. Part of the appeal of these showcases, from an agent's point of view, is the chance to see, en masse, well-trained young actors. As I mentioned, these showcases also draw the attendance of casting directors. Therefore, when later trying to promote these actors, agents realize there's a reasonable chance that a given casting director will have *also* already seen a particular actor's work, making the whole process an easier sell for the agent.

How much clout do these schools have? There can certainly be no question about the influence of "The Big Three." Broadway and off-Broadway productions are regularly peppered with actors from these specific programs, and certain schools seem to have certain clout in specific theatrical circles. New York University MFA graduates, for example, seem to scoot into the New York Shakespeare Festival with great regularity.

All told, the clout of the Big Three as potential entrée into the upper echelons of New York theater circles is undeniable. Does this guarantee longevity and a successful career? Nope. Is it necessary to go to these schools to have a chance? Only for those who truly believe that it is. There are many gifted and *ambitious* actors out there for whom the time further spent in academia (remember many of these programs are *graduate* programs) and/or the exorbitant tuition fees that often result in an enormous debt to carry into the beginnings of an insecure professional life are not feasible. However, it would be reasonable to suggest that regardless of one's training, the implementation of the strategies outlined heretofore can only enhance one's career opportunities.

Q: Besides the primary purpose of getting a job, and the ancillary benefits of building an arsenal of casting directors who know you, and having call-backs to report as progress reports, are there any other benefits to attending EPAs?

A: Absolutely. Many casting directors are casting several projects at the same time. If you're not quite right for one project, but you audition well, you may be considered for something else. Happens all the time.

Q: Any examples?

A: Here are a few recent ones. An actor I met had just taken over a role in a hit off-Broadway show. I asked her how she had gotten the part. She had attended an EPA for a different play a month before. She felt that she had auditioned exceptionally well, and was surprised when she wasn't called back. When the expected call finally came, it was for her to audition for another show, the one which she got. She *had* auditioned exceptionally well, but she was not the actor best suited for the part. But they had *not* forgotten her. Good casting directors have good memories for talented actors—that's part of what makes them good casting directors.

In another case, an actress had gotten a role on a television show from an EPA! How? The casting director of the play was the same person who cast the TV show! Many casting directors cast a broad spectrum of projects. Another actor came to me who had just auditioned for an EPA for an off-Broadway play. Three days later he found himself in the office of a soap's casting director reading for a new contract role. The soap's casting director had called the play's casting director and said, "If any guys fit the following description, and read well, please give me their names and phone numbers." I hear these stories all the time. That's why I say it's about being *out there.*

Q: Besides thorough preparation and selecting appropriate audition material, do you have any other suggestions for the monologue audition?

A: The casting process is, as we have said, a highly subjective one, but one thing I hear repeatedly from casting directors is that they want to be "surprised"; therefore I think it's the actor's job to be always searching for new, and fresh, material. You may be an excellent actor, but you'll be putting an enormous burden on yourself trying to "surprise" somebody with a piece they've seen eight hundred times. One good way to find material if you have a "prototype" who has worked a lot in the theater is to look this actor up in the indexes of John Willis's *Theatre World* or do an Internet search for a listing of this actor's body of work. You'll discover that this actor was in plays you've never heard of, or perhaps in plays you have heard of, in roles you never thought of for yourself, *until* you discover that this actor played this role. So *Theatre World* along with the Internet can make a good cross-reference of plays and actors. Another burden actors put on themselves is doing "story" pieces as monologues. By story pieces, I mean monologues where one character tells another character about something that has already happened. In the context of a well-written play, when one character tells another about something that happened, there is a *reason* why that character is telling the other character that story, *at that moment.* However, when an actor takes this story out of context of the play, the reason, or the need the "storyteller" has—to get something from the other character—usually goes out the window. Good actors often make poor choices trying to bring the story "to life." Look for material that is more "active," then, more in the moment, and more *involved* with the other character or characters in the scene. With many scenes you can edit out dialogue, or sections of dialogue, and create your own monologue. This "active" material, by its nature, is a more engaging choice.

Q: You've talked a lot about how to approach agents for representation for theater, film, and television. Does one approach agents for commercial representation in a different fashion?

A: Not really. You may, or may not, use a different photo selection, but the approach would be essentially the same. Unlike theater, however, one really must have an agent to get auditions for union commercials.

Q: How does one get started in television commercials?

A: Start by taking a really good on-camera commercial class. There are a number of good ones and they usually advertise in the trades. Audit or interview just as you would a theater class. Even though the current trend in commercial copy delivery is more toward the conversational and soft-sell, it is still advertising. Getting in a good commercial class will help you get into the advertising "frame of mind." Image, type, and learning to deliver copy on-camera are some of the things you'll learn.

Commercials are a great source of income that for some reason actors are sometimes unwilling to investigate. Often, an actor will say, "If I could work in film, I'd be able to afford to do theater." In most cases the amount of work one would have to do in film to give an actor the financial freedom to work in the theater would be at a pretty high career level, or at least in great regularity. Aiming at working in commercials would be a far more realistic expectation. Thanks to their income from commercials, many actors have been able to do low-paying stage work, which has boosted their career levels. In addition, filming commercials involves working with state-of-the-art cameras and equipment, top-notch directors and film crews, and doing many takes at many angles of the same scene many times. In short, working in television commercials is probably the best on-camera training one can get. Commercials are little movies.

Q: Does working in the theater help boost the commercial end of an actor's career?

A: Sure does. Commercial agents and casting directors are out looking for new faces, too.

Q: Are there any other benefits to attending a good on-camera commercial class?

A: There sure are. A lot of good schools also sponsor showcases with invited commercial agents and casting directors. This can be a good way to get seen. Commercials are, of course, advertising, and in general, commercial representation isn't quite as hard to get as theatrical representation.

Q: Can one implement the strategy of reporting commercial call-backs to commercial agents in the same way one reports film, television, and theater call-backs to agents who work in those areas?

A: By all means. In most cases, the commercial call-back comes in conjunction with something called the "first refusal." In essence, the first refusal means the advertising agency is asking you to hold the "avail" date—that is the shoot date—open for them, as they are considering hiring you. If you are not signed to one agency, and you get a first refusal, it's wise to tell other commercial agents about it on the photo postcard—it can increase your chances of getting more agents to work with you.

Q: Are the questions asked by television commercial agents in the agent/actor interview similar to the questions asked by agents who represent actors for theater, film, and television?

A: Very similar. For example, you will probably be asked, "Which *commercial* casting directors know you?" I've included a list that follows the same setup as the theatrical format. (See Appendix D.) Whoever hired you goes first, whoever *almost* hired you (call-backs and first refusals) goes next. Casting directors who have auditioned you, but never hired you or called you back, or put you on a first refusal, go next. *Exact* same format, exact same delivery on your part, when a commercial agent asks which casting directors know you. The "almost counts" theory is no less true with commercials than film, television, and theater. I stress keeping separate lists, however, as commercial agents and commercial casting directors are usually—but not always—different personnel from agents and casting directors who work in theater, film, and TV. If an agent in either area asks "which casting directors know you" (or know "your work"), don't respond with a mixture of names, unless you know that *both* the agent and the casting director whose names you mentioned work in the same areas. Often, I'll say to an actor, "Which casting directors know your work?" And the actor will respond, "Jeff Jones from *The Young Doctors* at ABC, Ann Smith at Blair Advertising . . ." Well, unless I am an agent working in both soaps *and* commercials—and *most* do not—this answer makes you look like you don't know what I do, and that you don't know what I need to know from you. Doesn't make you look too good. *If* you are not sure which areas an agent with whom you have a meeting scheduled works, check *Call Sheet* or check with the agency's receptionist *before* the day of the meeting. However you do it, make sure you know.

Q: You've proposed many more questions for the actor to pose to a personal manager than to an agent. Why is this?

A: Well, the main reason is because personal managers are not regulated in the way that franchised, licensed talent agents are. As I mentioned, agency contracts are much easier to get out of if you are not working, and they are usually signed for a shorter period of time. Also, we know that talent agencies are employment agencies, and we know that by checking with the unions, if we are a member, we can readily find out who else the agency represents. Not so with personal managers. So there is a need to ask more questions. And to be realistic, finding agency representation is, for most actors, *very* difficult. Unless one is being wooed by several agents, or is an in-demand actor who can pick and choose, for me to suggest all sorts of questions to pose to an agent would be naive. The main issues are: Do you and the agent see your casting and career possibilities in the same light? Is this agent enthusiastic? Is anyone else asking you to sign? The fact is, most actors do not, but would love to, have an agent.

Q: So then, there are no major concerns with respect to the agent/actor relationship?

A: Well, let me put forth a word of caution. Prospective representatives will often present a *best-case scenario* when asking actors to sign on, as in: "We see you as the next Brad Pitt or Julia Roberts, etc." However, representatives will work, as all good salespersons do, on a *worst-case scenario,* i.e., "What if that doesn't happen?" So, what do they do? Keep a hefty client list of fifty to a hundred clients just in case you *don't* become the Brad Pitt or Julia Roberts they have told you that you will become. Enthusiasm is essential, but don't let an agent (or manager for that matter) make your head swim with best-case scenarios. Like perfume, it's very nice to inhale, but you really don't want to swallow it. Consider this: If you're trying to sell your house, and you engage the services of a real-estate agent, does that mean your house is no longer your responsibility? Of course not. The same applies to your career. Therefore, protect yourself by thinking in terms of creating career-advancing opportunities and not handing over *all* the control to another party who will lose nary a wink of sleep if the promised best-case scenario doesn't come to pass.

Q: What do you see as the value—or lack of it—in the currently popular "paid" agent seminars? At these seminars agents are paid (from the actor's admission fees) to lecture, and then each participating actor performs.

A: In general, the value of these seminars will be in direct proportion to the combined elements of talent, age, looks, personality, and career level of the participating actors as they complement the current needs, taste, career levels, and areas represented by the agent who is being paid to conduct the seminar. More specifically, the results typically break down something like this. The greatest number of actors who benefit by such seminars do so in the area of representation for television commercials. Here's why.

First, the demand to cast faces of "unknowns" will always be greater for principal work in commercials—which are brief in length and concerned mainly with "type"—than to cast principal roles in major stage, television, and film productions. That is, casting directors—and therefore agents—for television commercials will generally be less concerned with the career level, credentials, and background of an actor than casting directors and agents of theatrical projects will be. In television commercials, it sometimes happens that the most important credit an actor needs in order to be granted an audition is a special skill—an athletic one, for example. This is not to say that commercial agents go out of their way to find actors who haven't trained, or that they don't represent actors already to whom they will usually give audition priority. It is simply to point out that an actor's credentials are not usually as important in the commercial world as they are in the theatrical world. "Theatrical" projects will usually require more substantial ability and, in most cases, weightier credentials on the part of the actor to be seriously considered for a given role. Furthermore, the ways in which the casting processes of these two areas are carried out are distinctly different in New York (although not in Los Angeles). Let's take a look at them.

When television commercials are slated to be produced by an advertiser in New York, the casting directors will, in almost all cases, contact *by email* only those agents with whom they wish to work. By email, the casting directors will tell the agents the specifics of what they are looking for in the way of actors. For a television commercial that is cast in New York, a pre-screen of photos and resumes is rarely required. (This is not the case in Los Angeles, however, where a photo and resume pre-screen *is* required by commercial casting directors. Unlike New York, commercial casting in Los Angeles is listed in *Breakdown Services*—the printed outline that agents subscribe to that gives the specifics of projects about to be cast.)

If a given New York agent gets the email, he or she already has the confidence of the casting director. Therefore, many or, in some cases, all of the actors suggested by this agent will often be granted an audition. So, then, if a good New York agent sees and wants to work with an actor— regardless of age—who has a particular look, energy, personality, and/or ability suited for television commercials, the agent will probably be able to secure an audition for that actor when the agent is working on a commercial "breakdown" for which that actor is suited.

However, casting directors for theatrical projects, in both Los Angeles *and* New York, almost always require agents to submit photos and resumes of those actors the agent wishes to be considered for an audition for a given project. These photos and resumes are then screened by the casting director and, subsequently, audition appointments are scheduled. Since all agents who subscribe to *Breakdown Services* are free to submit photos and resumes of their clients for any and all projects listed, casting directors ultimately get hundreds—and sometimes thousands—of photos and resumes for each project. In most but not all cases, casting directors will be more likely to want to see actors with the most substantial credits for these theatrical projects. In many cases, of course, they will even be looking for name actors. Logically, the more substantial the credits, the more likely it is that the casting director already will be familiar with an actor's career. Assuming too, that the actor is right for the role, the better his or her chances become of being considered for it. If we also consider the time factor required in the theatrical audition process—that is, setting up of audition appointments, first readings, call-backs, as well as the deadlines casting directors are up against—we can safely assume that the overwhelming majority of actors submitted by agents for theatrical projects subsequently will not be granted an audition.

If we would agree, then—for the above reasons—that theatrical representation is generally more difficult to get than commercial representation—on both coasts—where lie the benefits in "paid" agent seminars for *theatrical* representation? And what breed of actor gets them? As with so many other things in life, the young and the beautiful probably fare best, especially if they have talent. The younger the actor, the less is expected in the way of credentials on the resume. After all, if they're just starting out, why would their credentials be substantial? As I have said before, the pecking order of actors is not so rigidly observed with the very young actor.

The next group to benefit in the area of theatrical representation will be actors who have attained something in the way of substantial credits—whether these credits are from Broadway, off-Broadway, regional theater, or from film or television. While these actors may not be currently represented, their resumes might be strong enough for an agent to perceive them as "movable"—that is, able to compete with working actors who will also be submitted to casting directors for various projects.

This means that the older actor (which can mean anywhere from thirtyish and upward here) with *unsubstantial* credits will probably benefit the least in meeting agents for theatrical representation at such seminars. Generally speaking, the agent's feeling is likely to be that there are too many actors who are already known by the casting directors for this actor to realistically be able to compete in the casting process—*at least as it exists between agent and casting director.* Remember that casting directors get hundreds of pictures and resumes from agents, and only a small percentage of actors are usually granted an audition. Therefore, the actor who has done very little professionally—and is no longer especially young—will most likely be considered a "hard-sell" by most agents who represent actors for theater, film, and television. Please note: I am speaking about overall tendencies—not absolutes. *There will be exceptions.*

All of which means this. For the actor who does seek to meet agents and audition for them at seminars, I strongly suggest doing some homework prior to spending your money to meet with them. Again, I recommend a visit to IMDbPro.com to research an agency and its clients. How many actors' names do you recognize? What areas of the media do they work in? Can you get a sense of this agency's strengths? For example, some agencies have strong musical theater performers, others have several actors on daytime soaps, prime-time series, etc.

The New York actor should find out whether or not it is an agency's policy to work with freelance talent or on a signed-only basis—as is the standard policy in Los Angeles. In some, but not all cases, this means that the agency only accepts actors who are already somewhat established (exceptions being made for the young and the beautiful, of course!). In any event, if the agency works on a signed-only basis, it will mean that the number of actors with whom the agent can work will be fewer than if it is the agency's policy to freelance. This is certainly not necessarily a bad thing by any means, but it does reduce your chances of being able to work with a given agent. It could also mean that as much as an agent you meet likes you, he or she may still need to bring you in to meet his or her associates—who might *also* have to approve you before a working relationship can begin.

All told, be a smart shopper. Some establishments that sponsor these programs have a set list of guest agents; others allow actors to pick the agents they want to meet by signing up only for the specific seminars that these agents are conducting. Also, some establishments require an audition for an actor to be part of their program; others allow in all who wish to participate.

Last, but oh-so-far from least, one vitally important question. Are you agent ready? Are your audition skills and personal presentation such that an agent might want to invest in your career at this time? Get input from your teachers on this one. If you're not ready, don't go!

None of the above is meant to be an endorsement or a denigration of "paid" agent seminars. It is only an analysis of observations I've made as to who benefits the most and why. Still, I believe the best way for agents to see your work is in a more viable venue, such as a play, even though it can be difficult to get them to come. Therefore, for the actor who participates in seminars or is contemplating doing so, here is a suggestion. Be sure to *also* put your time and energies into advancing your career, building your resume, and sharpening your skills in the more established and time-honored fashion.

With all of the above having been said, let me conclude this discussion with a final observation: While many industry personnel have a deep understanding of their own area of the business, fewer have a broad understanding of the industry as a whole. As such, they are often prone to making sweeping generalizations and disseminating information that does not hold up in actual fact.

Q: You've talked a great deal about myths, excuses, reasons, awareness, specificity, making plans, forming strategies, getting control over your actions, and taking responsibility for your career. Any final words of advice?

A: Yes. Never ask an agent, casting director, or receptionist if you can borrow their stapler. Drives them crazy!

Appendix A

Name
Unions
website (optional)

Service/cell
email

Height: 5'11"
Weight: 165
Hair: Brown
Eyes: Blue

THEATER

Hard Times	Ray	Douglas Fairbanks Theater
The Fantasticks	Matt	Sullivan Street Theatre
Album	Billy	Cumberland Lane Stage (Cumberland, R.I.)
Mass Appeal	Mark	Foursquare Arts Center (Brighton, Mass.)
Equus	Alan	C. T. Jones Theatre (Lakeview, Maine)

TELEVISION

Guiding Light	Tommy (recurring)	CBS-TV

COMMERCIALS

On-camera principals for national network and regional usage (demo upon request)

TRAINING

Acting: Two-Year Meisner Technique program with Ron Stetson
Voice: Sara Krieger
Speech: Jean Lloyd
On-Camera Commercial Technique: Bob Thomas

SPECIAL SKILLS

Fluent German, saxophone, football, soccer, racquetball, golf, swimming, rock climbing, whitewater rafting

Appendix B

SAMPLE RESUME (LOS ANGELES FORMAT)*

Name
Unions
website (optional)

Service/Cell
email

Height: 5'7"
Weight: 125
Hair: Blonde
Eyes: Brown

FILM

| The Giant Within | Anne (supporting) | Touchstar Pictures (Jan Reed, Director) |

TELEVISION

Alias	Guest Star	ABC
Cold Case	Guest Star	CBS
The O.C.	Guest Star	FOX

THEATER

| Jenny Kissed Me | Jenny | Old London Rep Co. |
| Veronica's Room | Veronica | Boland Arts Festival |

THEATER

| Vanities | Joanne | Southwick Stage Co. |
| Biloxi Blues | Daisy | West Civic Theatre |

TRAINING

Acting: Jean Ann Edwards (Two years)
Speech: Tom Carlin
Dance: Jim Powers (ballet), Laura Roberts (jazz)

SPECIAL SKILLS

Piano, clarinet, oboe, aerobics, diving, gymnastics, tennis

* As film and television opportunities have increased in the New York market, this format is now often used in New York as well as in Los Angeles.

Appendix C

CASTING DIRECTOR	PROJECT	ROLE	AUD. DATE	RESPONSE	CB DATE
Jane Smith	The Seagull—Off-B'way	Treplev	6/1/09	CB'd for Dir. (Al Andrews)	6/4/09
Jane Smith	Diary of Anne Frank—New Haven Stage	Peter Van Daan	9/5/09	CB'd for Dir. (Lois Adams)	9/9/09
Jane Smith	The Sound of Music—Music Fair Tours	Rolf Gruber	4/4/09	CB'd for Dir. (Jim Ryan)	4/8/09
Jeff Jones	The Young Doctors—ABC-TV	Tim Donovan (recurring)	8/4/09	CB'd for Prod. (Ellen Thomas)	8/8/09
Betty Adler	Mass Appeal—Bridgeport Rep.	Mark Dolson	8/11/08		
Betty Adler	Biloxi Blues—Warren D. T.	Eugene Jerome	10/5/08		
Tom Roberts	The Matchmaker—Olney Stage	Barnaby	11/6/08		

Appendix D

TELEVISION COMMERCIALS
CASTING DIRECTORS WHO KNOW ME OR "KNOW MY WORK"

CD/ADVT. AGENGY	PROJECT	AUD. DATE	RESPONSE	CB DATE
Ed James Blair Advt.	Lemon-Up Soda	7/2/09	1st. Refusal for 7/9/09	7/6/09
Joan Mead Grant Advt.	All-Sports Sneakers	4/3/09	1st. Refusal for 4/10/09	4/6/09
Jill Harris Lee Advt.	Brazilian Coffee	2/3/09		
Jill Harris Lee Advt.	King's English Muffins	2/7/09		

Appendix E

American Theatre Magazine, published ten times annually by Theatre Communications Group, 520 Eighth Avenue, New York, New York 10018.

Back Stage, published weekly by Nielsen Business Media, Inc. 770 Broadway, New York, New York 10003.

Call Sheet, published six times annually by Nielsen Business Media, Inc. 770 Broadway, New York, New York 10003.

Directory of Theatre Training Programs, published by Theatre Directories, P.O. Box 159, Dorset, Vermont 05251.

The Hollywood Reporter, published by H. R. Industries, Inc., 5055 Wilshire Blvd., Los Angeles, California 90036.

L.A. Weekly, published weekly by L.A. Weekly, Inc., 3861 Sepulveda Blvd., Culver City, California. 90230.

The Regional Theatre Directory, published annually by Theatre Directories, P.O. Box 159, Dorset, Vermont 05251.

Show Business Weekly, published by David Pearlstein, 211 E. 43rd St., New York, New York 10017.

The Season Overview, published monthly by Rebecca Watson, 300 W. 49th St. #304, New York, New York 10019.

Theatre World, by John Willis, published annually by Applause Theatre and Cinema Books, 19 W. 21st St., New York, New York 10010.

Theatrical Index, published weekly by Price Berkley, 888 8th Avenue, New York, New York 10019.

Time Out New York, published weekly by Time Out New York Partners, LP, 475 Tenth Avenue, New York, New York 10018.

Appendix F

RECOMMENDED READING

Callan, K. *The Los Angeles Agent Book*. Studio City: Sweden Press, 2008.
———. *The New York Agent Book*. Studio City: Sweden Press, 2008.
Cohen, Robert. *Acting Professionally: Raw Facts About Careers in Acting*.
New York: McGraw Hill, 2003.
Decina, Rob. *The Art of Auditioning: Techniques for Television*. New York:
Allworth Press, 2004.
Donnelly, Kyle, ed. *Classical Monologues for Men*. Portsmouth, NH:
Heinemann, 1992.
———. *Classical Monologues for Women*. Portsmouth, NH: Heinemann,
1992.
Eaker, Sherry, comp. and ed. *The Back Stage Actor's Handbook*. New
York: Watson-Guptill/Back Stage, 2004.
Emory, Margaret. *Ask an Agent*. New York: Back Stage Books, 2005.
Lewis, M. K., and Rosemary R. *Your Film Acting Career*. Santa Monica,
CA: Gorham House, 1998.
Merlin, Joanna. *Auditioning: An Actor-Friendly Guide*. New York: Vin-
tage Books, 2001.
Searle, Judith. *Getting the Part*. New York: Limelight Editions, 1995.